George Waddle
Charlestown, Ind.

Rev. George T. Waddle

A CHURCH

ORGANIZED AND

FUNCTIONING

~~~

W. L. HOWSE

AND

W. O. THOMASON

Convention Press

NASHVILLE   TENNESSEE

Code Number: Church Study Course
This book is number 0105 in category 1, section
for Adults and Young People

Library of Congress catalog card number: 63-8299
Printed in the United States of America
5. AT 65 R.R.D.

ABOUT THE AUTHORS

WILLIAM L. HOWSE serves as director of the Education Division of the Baptist Sunday School Board, Nashville, Tennessee. He is a native of Fayetteville, Tennessee. He is married to Genevieve Morgan, and they have one son, William Lewis, III. Dr. Howse received the A.B. degree from Union University, the M.A. degree from Baylor University, and the M.R.E. and D.R.E. degrees from Southwestern Baptist Theological Seminary. Hardin-Simmons conferred the L.H.D. degree upon Dr. Howse in 1948. He holds the LL.D. degree from Union University, which was conferred in 1958.

Dr. Howse served as minister of education of the Broadway Baptist Church, Fort Worth (1927–30; 1935–45); Seventh and James Street Baptist Church, Waco (1930–32); Polytechnic Baptist Church, Fort Worth (1933–35); First Baptist Church, Dallas (1946); and University Baptist Church, Fort Worth (1947–49). Dr. Howse served as professor in the School of Religious Education at Southwestern Baptist Theological Seminary, Fort Worth, Texas, for twenty-two years. He has occupied his present position since 1954.

He is author of six books: *Teaching Young People in the Sunday School, In Spirit and in Truth, Guiding Young People in Bible Study, Sunday School and Missions, The Church Staff and Its Work,* and *Those Treasured Hours.*

WILLIAM O. THOMASON serves as assistant director of the Education Division, Baptist Sunday School Board, Nashville, Tennessee. He is married to Mary Roberts, and they have one daughter, Linda Cheryl. He is a native of Birmingham, Alabama. He received the B.S. degree from Auburn University and the M.R.E. and D.R.E. degrees from Southwestern Baptist Theological Seminary, Fort Worth.

He has also served as director of youth activities, Travis Avenue Baptist Church, Fort Worth, and as minister of education, Travis Avenue Baptist Church, Fort Worth (1951–53);

First Baptist Church, Muskogee, Oklahoma (1953–56); and First Baptist Church, Chattanooga, Tennessee (1956–58). Dr. Thomason was formerly editor of Nursery materials in the Sunday School Department, Baptist Sunday School Board. He has served in his present position since 1959.

He is coauthor of the book *Night and Day*.

PREFACE

THE AUTHORS are indebted to many persons for contributions made in developing the concepts expressed in this book.

Task Force III of the Baptist Sunday School Board was responsible for gathering and reporting much information from twenty-one churches regarding the functions of the church. Persons serving on this group included David K. Alexander, Ellis Bush, Eugene Chamberlain, Melva Cook, Clifford Holcomb, Crawford Howell, Nell Magee, Doris Monroe, Idus Owensby, Roger Skelton, and Maines Rawls. Members of study groups in the churches made invaluable contributions to the stating of these functions.

The following department heads of the Baptist Sunday School Board have stimulated thinking and made many helpful suggestions concerning the content especially as related to the areas of their responsibility: A. V. Washburn, Philip B. Harris, Howard B. Foshee, W. Hines Sims, E. Stanley Williamson, Joe W. Burton, David K. Alexander, Wayne Todd, Bob Boyd, and W. A. Harrell.

George Schroeder, secretary of the Brotherhood Commission, and Alma Hunt, executive secretary of Woman's Missionary Union, and members of their staffs have contributed liberally of their time and information to the development of the content of the manuscript.

Numerous other Southern Baptists, through their searching questions, led us to areas of thought and work heretofore neglected. Laymen, pastors, ministers of education, associational officers, SBC commission personnel, editors of state papers, state secretaries, and seminary professors have read this manuscript and commented on its adequacy for solving practical problems in our churches.

We wish to express appreciation to the staff of the Education Division office, who performed in an unusual manner in preparing the manuscript.

W. L. HOWSE
W. O. THOMASON

CONTENTS

CHURCH STUDY COURSE

THE CHURCH STUDY COURSE began October 1, 1959. It is a merger of three courses previously promoted by the Sunday School Board—the Sunday School Training Course, the Graded Training Union Study Course, and the Church Music Training Course. On October 1, 1961, the Woman's Missionary Union principles and methods studies were added.

The course is fully graded. The system of awards provides a series of five diplomas of twenty books each for Adults or Young People, two diplomas of five books each for Intermediates, and two diplomas of five books each for Juniors. Book awards earned previously in the Sunday School Training Course, the Graded Training Union Study Course, and the Church Music Training Course may be transferred to the new course.

The course is comprehensive, with books grouped into twenty categories. The purpose of the course is to help Christians to grow in knowledge and conviction, to help them to grow toward maturity in Christian character and competence for service, to encourage them to participate worthily as workers in their churches, and to develop leaders for all phases of church life and work.

The Church Study Course is promoted by the Baptist Sunday School Board, 127 Ninth Avenue, North, Nashville, Tennessee, through its Sunday School, Training Union, Church Music, and Church Administration departments; and the Woman's Missionary Union, 600 North Twentieth Street, Birmingham, Alabama; and by the respective departments in the states affiliated with the Southern Baptist Convention. A description of the course and the system of awards may be found in the leaflet "Trained Workmen," which may be obtained without charge from any one of the departments named.

A record of all awards earned should be maintained in each church. A person should be designated by the church to keep the files. Forms for such records may be ordered from any Baptist Book Store.

REQUIREMENTS FOR CREDIT IN CLASS OR HOME STUDY

IF CREDIT is desired for the study of this book in a class or by home study, the following requirements must be met:

I. IN CLASSWORK

1. The class must meet a minimum of seven and one half clock hours. The required time does not include assembly periods. Ten class periods of forty-five minutes each are recommended. (If laboratory or clinical work is desired in specialized or technical courses, this requirement may be met by six clock hours of classwork and three clock hours of supervised laboratory or clinical work.)

2. A class member who attends all class sessions and completes the reading of the book within a week following the last class session will not be required to do any written work for credit.

3. A class member who is absent from one or more sessions must answer the questions (pp. 145–46) on all chapters he misses. In such a case, he must turn in his paper within a week, and he must certify that he has read the book.

4. The teacher should request an award for himself. A person who teaches a book in the section for Intermediates or Juniors (any category) or conducts an approved unit of instruction for Nursery, Beginner, or Primary children will be granted an award in category 11, Special Studies, which will count as an elective on his own diploma. He should specify in his request the name of the book taught, or the unit conducted for Nursery, Beginner, or Primary children.

5. The teacher should complete the "Request for Book Awards—Class Study" (Form 150) and forward it within two weeks after the completion of the class to the Church Study Course Awards Office, 127 Ninth Avenue, North, Nashville 3, Tennessee.

II. IN HOME STUDY

1. A person who does not attend any class session may receive credit by answering all questions for written work as indicated in the book (pp. 145–46). When a person turns in his paper on home study, he must certify that he has read the book.

2. Students may find profit in studying the text together, but individual papers are required. Carbon copies or duplicates in any form cannot be accepted.

3. Home study work papers may be graded by the pastor or a person designated by him, or they may be sent to the Church Study Course Awards Office for grading. The form entitled "Request for Book Awards—Home Study" (Form 151) must be used in requesting awards. It should be mailed to the Church Study Course Awards Office, 127 Ninth Avenue, North, Nashville 3, Tennessee.

III. CREDIT FOR THIS BOOK

This book is number 0105 in category 1, section for Adults and Young People.

INTRODUCTION

IF THIS BOOK may be likened to a river, several streams of action as tributaries flow together to make it what it is.

In 1958, the Southern Baptist Convention, meeting in Houston, Texas, instructed its boards, agencies, and institutions to define their programs and to budget and report on them each year.

In carrying out the instructions of the Convention, those responsible for defining the educational programs at the Sunday School Board found it imperative to make a fresh study of the church and its basic tasks.

Twelve persons in the Education Division of the Sunday School Board were asked to devote nine months of their time to stating and defining the functions of the church. This task force met daily for several weeks to study the nature and functions of New Testament churches. Then members of the task force went in teams of two to twenty-one selected churches to study with them the functions of New Testament churches. As a result of this study the churches agreed that to worship, to proclaim, to educate, and to minister are functions of a church.

Another stream of action was the study of the program assignments of the Southern Baptist Convention to the Sunday School Board from 1845 to the present. The Historical Commission of the Southern Baptist Convention researched the material upon which this study was made. Using this information, the Convention agencies responsible for developing church educational programs, analyzed their work to make certain that all Convention assignments were included in their programs.

Another tributary to this book has been the development of a long-range planning service by the Church Administration Department of the Sunday School Board. This department, acting for the denomination, has worked with all Convention agencies in developing materials for church long-range planning.

The functions of a church formulated by the task force have been used as basic concepts in the development of these materials. Much valuable help has come from the pilot churches which have participated in the development of these materials and from resource panels representative of all Convention boards, agencies, and institutions.

These concurrent developments have contributed to the concepts which are represented on the pages of this book. These studies, all of which seem providential, are rooted in the New Testament and the historical assignments of the Southern Baptist Convention. At least one thousand persons have seen much, if not all, of this material in various forms. Those responsible for contributing to it are representatives of Southern Baptist Convention boards, agencies, and institutions; state secretaries; seminary professors; workers in the associations; pastors, church staff members; and volunteer workers in the churches.

The entire approach begins with the church as established by Christ and places it at the center of all planning and programing. It is in this context that the tasks of a church and its organizations have been stated so that a church may organize itself to function more effectively.

This book is being published with the expressed request that it not simply be thought of as another book, but as a manuscript in process of development. Please read and study the book carefully. It has been written with the earnest hope that it will provide *a* way, not necessarily *the* way, for a Baptist church to organize itself to function effectively.

We should like for this book to be representative of the concepts and opinions of Southern Baptist churches. We are particularly interested in your opinions if they differ with the concepts mentioned in the book. The principal objective of this book is to magnify the church, which Jesus establishes, and to strengthen it for its tremendous task and opportunity in our world.

A CHURCH ORGANIZED
AND FUNCTIONING

CHAPTER 1

I. THE NATURE OF A CHURCH
1. The Children of God
2. A Fellowship of Believers
3. The Body of Christ

II. THE FUNCTIONS OF THE BODY OF CHRIST
1. To Worship
2. To Proclaim
3. To Educate
4. To Minister

1

The Church
AND ITS FUNCTIONS

REVOLUTIONARY forces abound in our world today. Confusion, hatred, and fear are created by these forces. Turmoil, hate, and rebellion in individual lives and in nations cause many people to lose hope for the future of our world. This revolutionary spirit often motivates people to give their lives to ideas and causes that deny the very existence of God and the infinite worth of human personality.

Christ came into a world much the same as ours. He taught truth about God, man, righteousness, and evil. Having revealed truth, he reconciled evil man to God. He dispelled fear and gave hope to the hopeless. He placed infinite value on human life. Jesus commissioned those to whom he gave life to share this life and truth with others.

Christ established his church to counter evil forces in the world. In fact, first-century Christians were often called revolutionists. When Paul and Silas visited other Christians in Thessalonica, the Jews complained to the rulers, "These that have turned the world upside down are come hither also" (Acts 17:6). But as one has said, when Christians turn the world upside down, it is then right side up. Christ is continuing to establish and commission churches to enter into conflict with the evil forces that bring fear, hate, confusion, and rebellion to human life. Sharing his gospel is still man's hope for personal survival.

The challenge and opportunity of today demand that Southern Baptists understand clearly the nature and functions of their churches. Church members cannot understand the meaning of their church's existence unless they know who they are, what they are to do, and how they are to do it.

I. The Nature of a Church

The church owes its existence to God. It is his creation through Jesus Christ. The concept of the nature of a church held by the congregation influences the fulfilment of the true nature of a church. Therefore, it is imperative that this concept be scriptural.

1. *The Children of God*

A church is a congregation of the children of God. This is the interpretation given by the apostles and disciples of Christ. Consider the meaning of these words: "Behold, what manner of love the Father hath bestowed upon us, that we should be called the sons of God" (1 John 3:1).

A person becomes a child of God as a result of God's love in action. The manner of love the Father has bestowed upon us should not be taken lightly, for "while we were yet sinners, Christ died for us" (Rom. 5:8).

God's love is received by receiving his Son as Saviour and Lord. A church member can reshape his destiny and that of his congregation by understanding and applying the meaning of John 1:12–13: "But as many as received him [Christ], to them gave he power to become the sons of God, . . . which were born, not of blood, nor the will of the flesh, nor the will of man, but of God."

Being a son of God is a growing relationship. Each child is given the power to become a living, growing, new creation. Christian growth is essential on the part of the children of God. This becoming is more than the human striving of a church member or of a congregation. The Scriptures say: "For as many as are led by the Spirit of God, they are the sons of God. For ye have not received the

spirit of bondage again to fear; but ye have received the Spirit of adoption, whereby we cry, Abba, Father. The spirit itself beareth witness with our spirit, that we are the children of God: and if children, then heirs; heirs of God, and joint-heirs with Christ" (Rom. 8:14–17).

As children of God, we are called to reflect his nature in the world. As Christ revealed in his life the purpose of his coming, so should church members reveal the purpose for which God has called them: to be his children. To succeed in this, each person and each congregation must give continual attention to maintaining their relationship with God.

2. A Fellowship of Believers

Church members are not only children of God; they are also brothers in Christ. "In Christ" means to live in the reconciling love of God. Church membership is a brotherhood of love. This love cannot be understood in human terms alone. One must understand something of the love of God. "Herein is love, not that we loved God, but that he loved us, and sent his Son to be the propitiation for our sins. Beloved, if God so loved us, we ought also to love one another" (1 John 4:10–11).

The fellowship of love in a congregation of believers should be the most characteristic thing about a Baptist church. The New Testament writers spoke clearly regarding the necessity of this fellowship for the children of God. John said, "If a man say, I love God, and hateth his brother, he is a liar: for he that loveth not his brother whom he hath seen, how can he love God whom he hath not seen?" (1 John 4:20).

It is serious for a congregation to seek to function as the body of Christ when its fellowship has been broken or altered significantly. The command of Christ "that ye love one another, as I have loved you" involves more than an attitude. It is a command to establish and maintain a relationship of love with all other church members.

A church is a fellowship with Christ. The fellowship is

held together by Christ, for he is the common bond by which the fellowship is first created. He is the common bond by which the fellowship understands its purpose and by which the fellowship receives its power. It is to Christ only that a true church can give a common witness.

Paul wrote to the church at Galatia: "I am crucified with Christ: nevertheless I live; yet not I, but Christ liveth in me" (Gal. 2 : 20). When Christ dwells in the lives of church members, a unity of heart, mind, and purpose results; when Christ lives through the lives of church members, a fellowship beyond mere human experience develops. They are drawn together through his spirit to live his life.

Christians may engage in church activity, attend worship services, or carry out projects for their church without ever telling one another of their love for Jesus Christ. Is it not true that in the conversations of church members there is very little mention made of the Lord Jesus? Sharing Christ means bearing witness of his continuing action in a Christian's life.

A church cannot exist alone on the planned meetings which it holds. The congregation must share their heartaches, fears, hopes, and joys. The church must be present where life is lived. Sin is the mortal enemy of every congregation. The church must fear the results of sin and share in repairing the damages of sin as a part of this common life. Pride and false respectability are two attitudes which a fellowship of Christians cannot afford.

In answer to Thomas' question, "We know not whither thou goest; and how can we know the way?" Jesus answered: "I am the way, the truth, and the life: no man cometh unto the Father, but by me" (John 14 : 6). The word "way" includes the twofold idea of the route and the manner of going. The manner of going (living) was set forth by the sinless life which Christ lived. The Christians of the first century were often referred to as the people of the way because they sought to live apart from sin according to the example set by Christ.

A fellowship of "the way" is also a fellowship of self-denial. Going, giving, serving, choosing, and persevering are all a part of being in a community of true believers. The person who is unwilling to dedicate himself to this way of life is not ready to undertake his responsibility as a part of a Christian congregation.

3. *The Body of Christ*

A church is the body of Christ. In 1 Corinthians 12 : 27, Paul wrote, "Now ye are the body of Christ, and members in particular." God sent Jesus to carry out a mission that had been planned since the foundation of the world. While he was among men, Jesus established the church that it might continue this mission. He continues to establish churches toward this end.

Just as a physical body has many parts, so a congregation is a body with many parts. These parts are the individual members of the congregation. Not all have the same function, but they do have a single purpose. Individual members cannot fulfil their purpose except in relation to the other members of the church. Because the body exists for a specific purpose, God has given the individual members of a congregation the gifts or abilities which a church needs in order to perform its functions.

Often church members think that God has called only the pastor and other staff members. This idea is not true. Paul made clear in the fourth chapter of Ephesians that every Christian is called to a vocation in the body of Christ. His vocation is his work individually and as a part of the whole body. Failure on the part of a church member to find his place in the body of Christ makes the congregation less capable of carrying out the purpose for which it was established.

Christ is the head of the church. Charles B. Williams helps to make this clear through his translation of Ephesians 4 : 16: "For it is under His [Christ's] direction that the whole body is perfectly adjusted and united by every joint that furnishes its supplies; and so by the proper func-

tioning of each particular part there is brought about a growing of the body for its building up in love."

Meaningless activity is inconsistent with the life of Christ. Congregations need to evaluate the functions of the whole body to see whether its activity is contributing to the growth of the church and to the increase of love in the body of Christ. Just as a human body can waste time and energy and can misuse its members, so a church can waste time and energy and can misuse its individual members.

A congregation must give attention not only to itself as a whole body but also to its individual parts. Honoring some member of the body above others contradicts the teachings of the Scriptures (see 1 Cor. 12:12–31). Often the least honored member of a congregation, because of inadequate attention, gives the congregation most trouble. Or some member never achieves all that God intended because the body was too busy giving attention to its more honored members. Many congregations have not yet learned the truth of the Scriptures that "whether one member suffer, all the members suffer with it; or one member be honoured, all the members rejoice with it" (1 Cor. 12:26).

Churches are sometimes like people. Some are lazy; others are hard working. Some look for Christ's direction; others ignore Christ's leadership. Some think and pray and plan; others sit and argue and fail. God does not wait; the work of Christ is done by those who give attention to his will.

II. The Functions of the Body of Christ

Confusion exists in many churches as to what the work of Christ is. The Master was not confused; the New Testament indicates clearly basic functions of a church. The will of God for a particular congregation at a particular time can, of course, be known only as that congregation seeks God's will through prayer. But the responsibility of a church which seeks to pattern itself after the New Testament can be found in the functions to worship, to proclaim, to educate, and to minister. These functions are not in-

dependent of each other. Rather, they are interrelated and interdependent. As the lungs, heart, brain, and digestive system are vital to human life, worship, proclamation, education, and ministry are essential to the life of a church. Poor functioning in any one of these areas means a weak and limited body. Healthy functioning results in growth and effective working of the body.

1. *To Worship*

To worship is to experience an awareness of God, to recognize his holiness and majesty, and to respond in loving obedience to his leadership.

Essentially a worship experience is concerned with the creation and sustenance of life. All men stand in awe of life and the creator of life. From the beginning of time, man has worshiped the sun, the moon, the rain, and all other elements to which he has attributed life-giving powers. Christian worship is directed to Jehovah God, the source of eternal life. "But God, who is rich in mercy, for his great love wherewith he loved us, even when we were dead in sins, hath quickened us together with Christ, (by grace ye are saved)" (Eph. 2:4–5).

Worship is truly the heart of a church. Through it a congregation keeps in touch with God, the giver of life. Love, praise, repentance, and commitment are all genuinely and vitally expressed. Worship becomes more than a human fellowship. It is conscious personal fellowship with the conscious personal God as revealed in Jesus Christ.

The church worships God through praise, thanksgiving, and adoration. Remembering the mighty acts of God in Christ Jesus and his continuing work through the centuries, the church sings joyfully to God. The congregation bows in grateful thanksgiving for the grace of God that has made this possible. It reviews the work that God has done in its own life through the years, during the past week, and during the day.

Through the preaching and reading of the Scriptures, the church evaluates its life. It ceases to be selfish; it is called

to the true nature of a church. A worshiping church is a giving church, for it is impossible to worship without committing oneself to God. In worship, the congregation offers its love, its life, and its work to God.

Because God is present, worship is more than giving by the congregation. God also gives through worship. He gives the church the necessary strength for its life. Through the obedient congregation, God shares his power for living and growing, for loving and going.

The particular form of congregational worship depends upon each individual church. The essence of worship, however, is always characterized by several things: God is present and actively seeking a relationship with the congregation. The congregation is seeking to glorify God with one mind and one mouth (see Rom. 15:6). A worshiping congregation desires to know the truth in its deepest spiritual meaning. The Lord spoke of such worship when he said: "But the hour cometh, and now is, when the true worshippers shall worship the Father in spirit and in truth: for the Father seeketh such to worship him. God is a Spirit: and they that worship him must worship him in spirit and in truth" (John 4:23-24).

Worship calls for response on the part of the congregation. Many congregations are willing to watch the pastor and musicians perform. Often they sit waiting to see what will happen. But when the body of Christ is worshiping, every member makes a response to God. Singing is more than singing with the music director and the choir; it is singing to God. Praying is more than listening to the prayer leader; it is the entire congregation putting concern behind every word spoken. Listening to the sermon is more than listening to a preacher; it is seeking the truth of God through his revealed word. Many church members leave worship services tired from sitting rather than refreshed from worshiping.

Worship is never consummated until the worshiper serves. Obedient response is the essential criterion for judging the quality of a worship experience. "Thy will be done

in earth, as it is in heaven" (Matt. 6 : 10) is the response of every person who has truly worshiped. Thus worship is foundational to the church's effective witness in its immediate community and throughout the world.

2. *To Proclaim*

To proclaim the gospel is to declare what God has done in and through Jesus Christ for the salvation of men.

This is evangelism. Cut off the tongue of a church, and it will soon die. The last words Jesus spoke to his disciples were these: "After that the Holy Ghost has come upon you: and ye shall be witnesses unto me" (Acts 1 : 8).

Confronting unbelievers with the news that God has provided redemption from sin through Jesus Christ is evangelism. Churches which fail to declare this news are as branches that bear no fruit. In addition to witnessing to the unsaved, a church must deal with the doubts of church members until all "come in the unity of the faith, and of the knowledge of the Son of God, unto a perfect man, unto the measure of the stature of the fulness of Christ" (Eph. 4 : 13).

Preaching is a primary means for proclaiming salvation to the lost. Paul emphasized this when he wrote, "It pleased God by the foolishness of preaching to save them that believe" (1 Cor. 1 : 21). Preaching the gospel must take place where unbelievers are. Therefore, churches may need to reconsider their concept of preaching in order to reach those who do not come to the church building seeking God.

Proclaiming by a church is more than the preaching of the pastor. Every church member has a responsibility to fulfil this function. Personal witnessing about Jesus Christ is the day-to-day means by which a church proclaims. What God did in Jesus Christ, what Jesus Christ has done for men, and what God is doing today form the content of the proclaimed message to our world. Every person who has experienced salvation should be an evangel of God's grace.

The need of the world has not changed. Satan still dominates the hearts and lives of millions of persons. As evil

abounds, there is a greater need for the proclamation of the good news. Preachers have the major preaching responsibility in the life of a church, but the congregation cannot expect the preacher alone to proclaim the gospel to unbelievers. The preacher who must singlehandedly evangelize his community faces an almost impossible task. In addition, the church must invest in the missionary enterprise in the association, state, nation, and world.

Many congregations have excused themselves from their responsibility in evangelism. The New Testament teaches that all the members are to function as personal witnesses. Christ has not yet withdrawn his command for believers to be his witnesses. Churches must look anew at this function. They must develop the New Testament habit of sharing Christ each day.

3. *To Educate*

From the Christian standpoint, to educate is to lead persons to the knowledge and acceptance of the Christian faith and life, to train church members to perform the functions of their churches, and to motivate them in Christian living and service.

Although persons may be taught concepts of the Christian life, education in it begins with the conversion experience. Learning in the Christian life is essential to the growth of every redeemed person. Education is the process by which persons grow in understanding, form new attitudes, and develop actions consistent with the example of Christ. This learning is aided by the work of the Holy Spirit.

Christian growth is dependent upon the processes of learning just as physical growth is dependent upon the digestive processes. Christ set the example for a church in education. He spent most of his time teaching. His invitation to the multitudes was: "Take my yoke upon you, and learn of me; for I am meek and lowly in heart: and ye shall find rest unto your souls" (Matt. 11:29).

It was the pattern of the New Testament churches to educate. All those who were added to the church were expected

to "continue steadfastly in the apostles' doctrine" until they had been stabilized in the Christian faith and life. Paul urged the Christian to walk "rooted and built up in him [Christ], and stablished in the faith," as they had been taught (Col. 2:7). The searching mind, seeking for the truth of God, is the clearest evidence that a person is growing toward Christian maturity. The words of Christ "Ye shall know the truth, and the truth shall make you free" should cause every church to undertake its educational function with renewed strength and purpose.

Through education Baptist churches learn how to be churches. Actually, each church is a school. In addition to being a school, it must have schools. In other words, the church educates in an informal and in a formal manner. This statement recognizes that much of the education of a church takes place in the life of the congregation, for every action of a congregation has in it educational consequences. It is the responsibility of the congregation to see that education, informal and formal, contributes to significant learning experiences on the part of its members.

Since some learning takes place outside the church and its classrooms, the congregation should look upon experiences such as birth, death, marriage, and sickness as particularly valuable opportunities for Christian education.

In order to be sure that learning is meaningful, Baptist churches need to identify the study programs which they must carry on. A study program is any basic area of content which requires continuing study on the part of the congregation if the church is to achieve its objectives. The study programs of a church must provide opportunities for the congregation to learn about every aspect of the Christian faith and life. The studies must provide depth that will stabilize the believer thoroughly in the faith. They should also prepare him to live as a world citizen. The following study programs exist in most, if not all, Baptist churches today:

Biblical revelation
Systematic theology and ethics

Christian history
Christian music and hymnody
Church polity and organization
Performance of the functions of a church
Education principles and methods
Administration principles and methods

The definition and relationship of each of these will be discussed in subsequent chapters.

4. *To Minister*

Many times during his ministry Jesus' body was tired and exhausted. On more than one occasion it was necessary for him to withdraw from the multitudes to seek a place of isolation. Yet no man has ever lived who had the compassion or who felt the suffering of mankind as did Jesus. Day after day of his short life was spent ministering to the sick, the lame, the sad, and the hungry.

Jesus taught what he expected from those who would become his disciples. He set a clear standard by which a person might measure importance or status as a member of the body of Christ: "But whosoever will be great among you, let him be your minister; and whosoever will be chief among you, let him be your servant: even as the Son of man came not to be ministered unto, but to minister, and to give his life a ransom for many" (Matt. 20:26–28).

As congregations grow, it is easy for Christians to become insensitive to the suffering, loneliness, and physical needs of fellow members and persons in the community or around the world. With community welfare agencies undertaking more and more social action, churches find it easy to forfeit their function of ministry. Congregations must awaken to the consequences of ignoring Christ's warning about the final judgment. Read Matthew 25:42–46, and consider especially these words: "For I was an hungred, and ye gave me no meat: I was thirsty, and ye gave me no drink: I was a stranger, and ye took me not in: naked, and ye clothed me not: sick, and in prison, and ye visited me not. Then shall they also answer him, saying, Lord when saw

we thee an hungred, or athirst, or a stranger, or naked, or sick, or in prison, and did not minister unto thee? Then shall he answer them, saying, Verily I say unto you, Inasmuch as ye did it not to one of the least of these, ye did it not to me."

Ministering to a person's needs is another way to witness of Christ, for ministering is making a loving response to the needs of persons in Jesus' name. To serve for selfish reasons is worse than not serving at all. The Christian's integrity is weakened when he serves from selfish motives. Christians are servants of Christ and, therefore, servants of all men in need.

A church is the body of Christ and as such should follow his example. It must ask itself what it will do about the hungry and suffering of the world. Congregations must learn to suffer with mankind wherever suffering takes place.

Foreign missions and home missions give opportunity for churches to co-operate in sharing the burdens of men of every race in every nation of our world. But giving gifts to be used by others is not enough. Churches must share personally the common life struggle.

Ministry may be expressed individually or collectively. In ministering individually, a person may seek to meet the physical need of someone, as did the good Samaritan, or he may seek to meet a spiritual need, as Jesus did in personal witness to the woman at the well. Individual ministry may be expressed as members engage in personal or group counseling or as they visit in homes.

Collective ministering may be expressed in such actions as sharing clothes with the needy or food with the hungry. A church may make benevolent responses to those who are homeless, financially distressed, or transient. Collective ministry may be expressed in attention to special groups with particular needs, such as language groups, racial groups, military personnel, or students.

CHAPTER 2

2

The Task of
THE CONGREGATION

UNDERSTANDING the nature and functions of a church is the beginning point as a church organizes itself for work. With this knowledge for a basis, a church determines the action necessary to carry out its work. It learns the tasks to be done; then it organizes to perform them.

Organization, although characteristic of churches since New Testament days, is quite often misunderstood. When a congregation lacks an understanding as to why an organization exists, there is a tendency to magnify the organization itself. The organization that does not exist as a means for accomplishing significant and important goals becomes an end in itself. In such a case, it is possible for the will of God to become subordinate to an organization.

Church organization is the way whereby members relate themselves to one another for accomplishing specific church tasks. An organization should be evaluated on the basis of the help it gives the church in functioning successfully.

The initial step as a church organizes is to determine those tasks performed by the congregation as a whole. There are certain things which a Baptist congregation must do because of its nature. Until it has identified these tasks and stated its purpose in regard to them, a congregation is not ready to assign other tasks of the church or to bring organizations into being.

The tasks which a congregation may assume for itself will depend, of course, upon many factors. Size, location, leadership, and financial resources are some of the factors which will influence this decision. The following, however, seem to be tasks which every congregation must assume and must be educated to carry out as a body if it is to be truly a congregational church.

I. Responsibility to Be a New Testament Church

The nature and the basic functions of a church have been considered. The conclusion might be drawn that a church is a church and that nothing can change its nature. This conclusion is not true. Churches cannot attain the objectives Christ set forth, but they can press toward the mark. Striving toward this goal is the surest evidence that a church is truly a church. Every congregation, if it is a true church, must evaluate itself under the leadership of the Holy Spirit. Seeking answers to the questions Are we the children of God? Are we a fellowship of love? Are we the body of Christ? may give direction to the congregation in its efforts to become the church that it was meant to be. Such answers require the leadership of the Holy Spirit and time for searching.

II. Responsibility to Participate

A church, if it is to be a true church, cannot neglect to worship, proclaim, educate, and minister. These functions are not just the responsibilities of individuals; they are the actions of the entire body. Many members of Baptist churches "hold membership in" rather than "belong to" the church. Some persons feel that they have the right to decide what they will do and what they will not do. No one should deny the right of any individual to interpret the will of God for his own life. Nor should any child of God who understands his relationship to the body of Christ deny the claim which the church has upon each member.

A congregation must recognize that not every activity is a function. The word "function" means the natural,

proper, or characteristic action of a thing. In this case, function would mean the essential actions of a church without which its true nature would be altered. Many activities carried on by churches today are good, and they contribute to its personal welfare. They are not, however, necessarily essential to its nature. Many activities are planned to meet the needs of only a part of the membership. Whatever else it does, the congregation as a whole must worship, proclaim, educate, and minister.

This concept of congregational responsibility requires a congregation to take a careful look at the way in which its basic functions are performed. There is more than one way for an action to be carried out. A method used a few years ago may now have become obsolete and ineffective. As a church grows, it may need to change its ways of doing things. The church must plan its life and work to reflect the uniqueness and individuality of its congregation. The problems of individual members, families, and the congregation need to be reviewed. On the basis of this information, the church should plan its life and work. Having done so, a congregation has a right to expect all members to participate in basic functions of the church.

For example, the church that decides to operate only a Sunday school must face the question of how to do the total educational task of the church. If a church does not provide an Extension department in its Sunday school, it must face the question of how church members unable to come to the church building will be involved in the life and work of the church.

III. Responsibility to Govern

Baptist churches have always taken pride in being spiritual democracies. Congregational government, based upon the doctrine of the priesthood of the believer, has been a distinctive practice of Baptist churches. Such government has the primary objective of directing affairs of the church for the best spiritual interests of individual members together with the membership as a whole.

True congregational government has often suffered as some Baptist churches have grown too large for the congregation to make all decisions regarding its work. When congregational government is displaced by another form of government, it has usually been the result of drifting rather than voting to change the manner of operation.

Creative action on the part of the congregation is needed to solve this problem, for congregational government requires continual attention to prevent its perversion. Education in the congregational processes of government is an absolute necessity for Baptist church members. That is why the study of Baptist polity must be given continual attention in the learning opportunities provided by the church.

If a church is to maintain the integrity of its congregational government, it must determine its own course of action, provide resources, and select leaders. Having taken these actions, the church must continually evaluate the work it is doing in terms of the objectives it has set.

Every church member is responsible for participating intelligently in the democratic actions of the congregation. Such participation requires members to understand the nature and objectives of the church, the relationship of a particular action to the objectives of the church, and arguments for or against the action. Each member should prepare himself through worship to do the will of God and to maintain the fellowship of the church.

IV. Responsibility to Determine Its Course

Since some activity or actions of a church may not be essential, it is imperative that a congregation determine what it is trying to do.

1. *Determine Its Objectives*

A statement of this determination could become the objectives of the church. With a statement of objectives as a point of orientation, the congregation can then decide which actions will contribute most to the achievement of these objectives.

A church that has set objectives is ready to determine which actions contribute to the progress of the church. Members should have opportunity to express regularly, under the direction of the Holy Spirit, their insights and evaluations about the work of their church.

Conflict arises in Baptist churches when congregations consider matters which are not basic before they have stated their basic, continuing objectives. For example, the church that has accepted the basic task of reaching the lost for Bible study has committed itself to a program. This consists of additional activities such as providing trained leadership, adequate buildings, visitation, and an enlarged organization. When the basic task has been assumed, the matter of providing the other means has been settled. The decision to accept the basic task with all related responsibilities does not rule out the matter of the congregation deciding how or when these other actions will be taken.

Churches need to set forth their intentions in stewardship, evangelism, missions, and other areas where they expect to be taking action year after year. Just as a church finds unity of spirit in Christ, setting objectives can give a church unity in its action.

Congregational government can be exciting when it is concerned with weighty matters. Involving all church members in determining what the church will do also educates them for responsibility. Significant learning can take place in properly conducted church business meetings. Spirit-led seeking, intelligent discussion, questioning, referral of matters for further study in a fellowship of brotherly love should characterize a church as it determines its course through congregational action.

A congregation should develop a statement of objectives. This statement will reflect in a formal way its intentions. One church states its objectives this way:

1. To experience an awareness of God's presence, and to respond in loving obedience through worship
2. To proclaim the mighty acts of God in Christ Jesus
3. To educate in the Christian faith and Christian life

4. To minister in Jesus' name through responsible action in meeting the needs of all persons
5. To determine the constituency which the church is to seek to serve
6. To provide programs, leaders, and facilities for a resident membership of _____ persons
7. To provide program and administrative services suitable to the church's functions, constituency, and size

2. *Determine Its Programs and Services*

Baptist churches believe that the congregation should determine by majority consent the course of action it will take. The congregation should authorize and establish programs, program services, and administrative services. A program is any major continuing activity which has primary importance in achieving the basic objectives of the church. For example, the seven tasks of the Sunday school, listed in chapter 4, grouped together form the Sunday school program.

A **program service** is any major continuing activity that exists to enrich or aid programs in achieving the basic objectives of the church. For example, the library provides books to enrich and aid in teaching the biblical revelation or in training church members to perform the church's functions.

An **administrative service** is any major continuing activity that exists to serve those who direct and guide the work of the church. For example, the nominating committee exists to provide leadership for the Brotherhood president, the Sunday school superintendent, and other organizational leaders. The finance committee exists to provide a budget and finances for Woman's Missionary Union, Training Union, church office, et cetera. When the church has properly authorized the establishment of one of the above services, it has determined that certain leadership positions will be created.

V. Responsibility to Provide Resources

Every Baptist church has resources and means for doing

its work. The resources of a church include the Holy Spirit, talents, money, and facilities. God provides the Holy Spirit; the congregation with God's help must provide the others. The congregation must call forth from its members those resources needed to do its work.

This response is Christian stewardship. This kind of stewardship requires a commitment to Christ and to his work. Christian stewardship is the church member's commitment to the body of Christ and its work in the community and around the world. One's commitment to this work involves his time, talent, and money.

No apology should be made for asking people to do the work of the church. Calling people to tasks in the church is a call from self-centeredness. It is an invitation to participate in congregational action.

Poor administration of the resources of the church leads to misunderstanding and dissatisfaction on the part of members. Some persons feel that they are being misused by the church, and in some cases they are. Serving the congregation in a place of responsibility is more than becoming a tool of the church. A congregation has a holy responsibility to see that its human resources are used wisely.

The congregation is equally responsible for providing the financial resources and physical facilities for the work of a church. Giving money, providing buildings, and supplying equipment should be a spiritual experience. A well-planned interpretation of how and why thousands of dollars of the church's money will be used can make budget pledging a valuable educational experience. When a church considers constructing a new building, months are usually devoted to discovering and sharing the reasons why the building is needed, why it should be a certain size, why it should be constructed of certain materials, and why it should be designed a certain way. In comparison, a church will often present its annual budget with a few simple headings and a few figures. After minimum discussion the congregation is asked to vote on a budget that equals in amount of money that which would erect a building.

Church members should understand why a budget is needed. Commitment to give to the budget should be a commitment to sustain the life and work of a church. When this is understood, giving money and providing buildings can and should be a major spiritual experience in the life of the congregation.

VI. RESPONSIBILITY TO SELECT LEADERS

Guidance is necessary if a church's objectives are to be reached. Leaders have the responsibility for giving direction and guidance to the work of the church. Choosing persons to lead the congregation is an important action of the church.

The selected person understands the congregational action to mean that he is serving his church. Of course, the congregation likewise establishes the organizations through which leaders work. Each leader must realize that he is ultimately responsible to the congregation and to God for the work which he does.

Selection of leaders is not a trivial action. A mistake at this point can be disastrous. Many problems which disrupt fellowship and split churches could be avoided if congregations approached the task of selecting leaders more seriously. The blind attitude that anybody can do anything contradicts the teachings about the members of the body of Christ as found in the New Testament. An eye is not a hand, nor is a hand a foot. One leader is not the same as another leader. One job does not require the same ability and personality that another requires. Congregations should not be a party simply to putting people to work. Selecting leaders is a holy act. Certainly it was to the Antioch church which set apart Paul and Barnabas to do the work of that church among the Gentiles. So it should be to Baptist churches today.

The practice of annual election of church leaders is the normal procedure in most Baptist churches. This action by the congregation should be properly understood as the best time to get the right people in the right places of service.

If a church has made an error in the preceding year, then it should take steps to correct the situation at this time.

Refusal to re-elect is seldom the best way to handle a worker who has not succeeded in his assignment. Annual election should be a time to review with an individual his efforts and to call him to a higher level of service. Christians are often hesitant to discuss the weaknesses of another. This evaluation can be a means for Christian growth when done in Christian love and in the proper manner.

Annual election should be a time of recommitment on the part of every worker who is to serve the church for the coming year. It is a time for each to dedicate himself to improving his leadership abilities. It is the time for leaders to take a new look at what the church is trying to do and to lead creatively toward this goal. Congregations should develop a policy of selecting leaders that takes into account the nature and functions of the church and the worth and capability of each person.

The selection of ministers and other church employees requires special skill, as well as the direction of the Holy Spirit. A representative group is not the only criterion to be considered in establishing a pulpit or personnel committee. The question is not whether the prospective worker will please youth or adults. The question is whether this person can fulfil the responsibilities of the job to which the church is calling him. The committee members need to understand the nature of their church, the real desires of the congregation, and the problems which will confront a person who is called as pastor or employee of the church.

In addition to leadership tasks, a minister must have opportunity to express the special gifts which have been given to him by the Holy Spirit. Selection of a pastor, minister of education, or minister of music by the congregation should include a commitment by the congregation to grant these persons freedom to work under the direction of the Holy Spirit. A church that is unwilling to grant this freedom has no right to call a minister to leave his pastorate and become their servant in Christ.

CHAPTER 3

I. Responsibilities of the Pastor and Church Staff
1. Perform Pastoral Functions
2. Minister Through Administration

II. Responsibilities of Deacons

III. Responsibilities of Church Officers and Committees
1. Plan, Conduct, and Evaluate
2. Recommend
3. Report

IV. Legal and Formal Means for Conducting Church Affairs
1. Church Constitution
2. Church Business Meeting
3. Trustees
4. The Church Council
5. Organizations and Officers

V. Recommending and Reporting to the Congregation

3

The Task of
CHURCH LEADERS

CARRYING ON the work of a church smoothly and effectively requires administration. The basic meaning of the word "administration" is theological. It means "to minister." The ministry of administration is to direct people as a group to achieve spiritual goals. Leaders in a Baptist congregation should try to use democratic processes. Such administration is based upon the assumption that a congregation under the direction of God is self-responsible, self-directing, self-understanding, and free to outgrow its immaturity resulting from ignorance and unbelief.

Democratic administration recognizes that authority to operate must come from the consent of the majority. This principle is sometimes hard for church leaders to accept because they are often able to see the correct or better way more clearly than the church members they lead. They are responsible for seeing further than the congregation. Patience in accepting the principle of authority by majority consent, however, is the surest way of keeping the church unified and moving toward its goals. The leader may have to sacrifice his personal goals in order to maintain the unity of the congregation. Willingness to do so requires maturity on the part of church leaders. On the other hand, leaders must not be content to sit idly by simply because the congregation does not want to move. If Moses had decided to

move only when the children of Israel desired to do so, it is likely that their journey would have lasted longer than forty years.

Democratic administration is more of an ideal than a reality. Since imperfect people make up the congregation and serve as leaders, they must always strive to understand more clearly the democratic processes. A person who serves as an administrative leader in a church will make errors at times. These errors may disturb the fellowship of the church. Therefore, every member of a congregation must be willing to forgive errors of administrative judgment just as they forgive moral or spiritual sins. To the degree that Christian love is present, democratic processes are effective.

A congregation must decide upon the number of offices which it will establish. The following factors influence this decision: the number of members in the congregation; the number and extent of programs the congregation authorizes; the leadership resources available; and, in the case of employed leaders, the amount of finances available. Some offices call for ordained persons; others will be filled by lay members of the congregation. The honor a particular office receives depends upon the service rendered. The ordained officers of the church should possess special gifts for ministering to the congregation.

In 1926, English Baptists adopted a reply to the Lambeth Appeal. The Baptist reply still represents the convictions of most Baptists, not only in England but throughout the world. The following is quoted from the reply of 1926:

Our doctrine of the Church determines our conception of the ministry. We hold firmly the priesthood of all believers, and therefore have no separated order of priests. The ministry is for us a gift of the Spirit to the Church, and is an office involving both the inward call of God and the commission of the Church. We can discover no grounds for believing that such a commission can be given only through an episcopate, and we hold that the individual Church is competent to confer it. For us there is no more exalted office than a ministry charged with preaching the Word of God and with the care of souls. Yet any full description of the ministerial functions exercised

among us must also take account of other believers who, at the call of the church, may preside at the observance of the Lord's Supper or fulfil any other duties which the Church assigns to them. [1]

I. RESPONSIBILITIES OF THE PASTOR AND CHURCH STAFF

The pastor is expected to be gifted in preaching the gospel and in performing special ministries to or for the congregation. In addition, the office of the pastor carries the responsibility of serving as chief administrator of the church.

1. *Perform Pastoral Functions*

The congregation expects the pastor to exercise his gift of preaching. They expect him to preach with authority the Word of God to the congregation in a manner that will bring salvation to the lost and will challenge believers to spiritual growth.

A congregation likes to share the preaching of their pastor with the whole community. If he is preaching the Word of God effectively, church members will tell others and will invite them to hear him. The community in which a church is located expects the pastor to preach the Word of God, and they respect him for his work. "How beautiful upon the mountains are the feet of him that bringeth good tidings, . . . that publisheth salvation" (Isa. 52:7).

A pastor best reflects Jesus Christ when he is ministering to persons at a time of special need. His presence in time of birth, sickness or death, allows him to share the deepest emotions of the members of his congregation. No other person in a church has this privilege. Such a ministry creates a bond between the pastor and the congregation—a bond of love, of understanding, and of Christian fellowship. Out of such occasions is built the relationship which permits the pastor to counsel with a church member who has personal problems, to exhort the wayward member, and to admonish

---

[1] Quoted in A. C. Underwood, *A History of the English Baptists* (London: Carey Kingsgate Press, Ltd., 1947), p. 262. Used by permission.

the slow of heart. Without this ministry, it is impossible for the pastor to fulfil his total responsibility.

Modern living has made this ministry of the pastor more essential than ever. Our congregations must help their pastors find a way to perform this special gift which God has given to them. Through his ministry the pastor sets the example for the congregation to follow in ministering to the needs of one another and in extending the ministry of the church into the world. The world has never been able to reject the witness of Christian love.

2. *Minister Through Administration*

Administration is directing people to achieve a goal that is commonly agreed upon. It is the process of uniting the efforts of people so that a desired result is achieved. An administrator is responsible for both actions and results. Administration in a Baptist church, however, is more than just directing or uniting the efforts of people. Administration is a ministry to the total personalities of those being directed or united. The Christian administrator has the responsibility of leading people to use their energies and abilities to achieve the very best for their lives. He must seek diligently to aid persons to reach their highest levels of performance. He must lead the ten-talent man to be a ten-talent man and at the same time assure the one-talent man that his efforts are just as necessary and valuable to the group as a whole. The true administrator is always calling— calling God's people to become each day more of what God intends them to be.

(1) *Pastor.*—As chief administrator of the congregation, the pastor is responsible for over-all actions and results in the work of the church. In fulfilling this responsibility, the pastor leads the church to worship, proclaim, educate, and minister. He tries to lead all members of the body to share the common objectives and purposes of the congregation. A pastor's administrative responsibility is to lead persons away from the things of the world and into the high calling of Christ Jesus.

This responsibility of the pastor demands that he have a clear understanding of the nature and functions of a Baptist church. Also he needs skill in planning, overseeing, and evaluating the efforts of the church. He should have the ability to decide upon the best course of action.

A pastor needs to understand and to practice the art of delegating responsibility. The wise pastor is one who shares church activities and responsibilities with others. In so doing, he not only extends his own work and accomplishes more but also involves many other persons in the life and work of the church. Some pastors have learned the joy that comes from sharing with others the menial and major tasks in the kingdom of Christ. Such administrative action may require more time, more skill, and more effort; but it strengthens the work of the church.

Some churches have grown so large that more than one minister is needed. In such cases the pastor must serve as a leader of other staff members. The work of such ministers or staff members consists of responsibilities that originally belonged to the pastor. The work of the laity should not be assigned to an employed staff member. To do so would in time weaken the church. Ministers who share the work of the pastor should try to multiply the efforts of the church members through leading them to more effective service.

(2) *Other administrators.*—There are many tasks which a pastor can share with others. For instance, the minister of education or the minister of music helps the pastor get his tasks done by leading the program of education or music. These colaborers free the pastor for other service to the church. Having these helpers does not, however, give the pastor more time. It is a well-known fact that supervising other people requires time. The pastor is responsible for leading these persons to minister to the congregation. They, too, must understand the objectives and programs of the congregation. They must understand how their ministry and the programs they lead contribute to the total work of the church. The pastor and staff members must evaluate work that is done to be sure that it is harmonious with the objec-

tives of the church. The pastor must teach church staff members how to use their offices in a spiritual manner.

Baptist churches have established many offices in order to conduct their work. Deacons and program leaders of the Sunday school, Training Union, Music Ministry, Woman's Missionary Union, and Brotherhood look to the pastor for leadership. In him they see the objectives of the church personalized. He inspires and motivates them to accomplish the work they have been selected to do. He provides counsel that will keep the work of each organization properly centered in the purposes of the church. He helps to develop in the leaders the qualities, skills, and attitudes which they need in order to serve effectively in their situations.

Certainly the pastor should love those he leads. He does not use them just to accomplish results for himself or for the church. He helps them find the full meaning of life through the work the church has selected them to do.

The pastor is also concerned for the life of the congregation. He is responsible to lead in the use of the resources of the church to the best advantage. Success requires coordination, wise planning, and the ability to make the decision that some activities and meetings are more vital than others to the work of the church. The pastor who fulfils the role of leader in his church may be required to express courageous leadership in the face of opposition. If such a role is necessary, he should be willing to accept it.

II. RESPONSIBILITIES OF DEACONS

The office of deacon had its beginning in the days of the apostles. Finding themselves overburdened with everyday matters while seeking to preach the gospel, to administer the functions of the body of Christ, and to minister to the members, the apostles asked the church for assistance. The first helpers waited on tables and made decisions regarding the distribution of food. Just as the office was established to assist the apostles, deacons in Baptist churches today are chosen to assist the pastor in doing his work. They should support his preaching ministry. At times, they, too, like the

New Testament deacons, should preach the word of God.

Deacons are not the rulers of the church. Rather, they are called to minister. The word "deacon" is derived from the Greek word *diakonia,* which originally meant one who waits on tables. The word *diakonos* came to mean servant in the New Testament church. Performing personal ministries to all the members of a congregation is a major task for many pastors. The larger the congregation, the more difficult the task. Pastors and deacons need to share responsibility in this work. They have as their primary responsibility the welfare of church members. Scriptural qualifications for deacons demand that they be men of the highest spiritual and moral quality. This requirement is necessary if they are to perform the spiritual ministry of their office. Deacons should be the most prayerful and the most deeply concerned group in a church.

III. RESPONSIBILITIES OF CHURCH OFFICERS AND COMMITTEES

Most Baptist churches select church leaders to give direction to established programs. Some of these are the Sunday school superintendent, Training Union director, Woman's Missionary Union president, and Brotherhood president. In addition to these leaders, the church may have a moderator, a clerk, a treasurer, trustees, and committees. Whatever the office, the persons are selected to administer certain areas of the church's work.

1. *Plan, Conduct, and Evaluate*

The congregation selects leaders to direct its programs, program services, and administrative services. These leaders are responsible to the congregation for the actions and the results in their assigned areas. Planning, conducting, and evaluating are actions which characterize the work of these leaders. Planning is determining the future action necessary to accomplish specific goals. It includes determining which actions are of greatest importance and when such actions should take place. Conducting is carrying out according to

plan the action or actions that have been developed. Evaluating is the review of what has been accomplished toward desired goals and judging the value of past actions.

Program leaders are responsible for planning the work of their organizations. Furthermore, they are expected to do the work necessary to carry out their plans successfully. They are responsible for evaluating the effectiveness of their work and for reporting achievements to the congregation.

A wise administrator knows the value of planning and evaluating the work for which he is responsible. Does the Sunday school in your church operate the same way it did thirty years ago? Is the Training Union the same size it was a decade ago? The answer to these questions will indicate whether the leaders are doing more than operating their programs. Progress comes as a result of planning. Improvement is the result of evaluation. If church programs are not functioning properly, perhaps it is because creative leaders are not devoted to solving the problems.

2. *Recommend*

The program leader is responsible to the congregation for recommending goals for his program. Goals are the desired outcomes a leader expects to achieve through specifically planned actions. A church may have known originally why it established a certain organization. Time, however, brings changes. People forget why a thing was done. The nature of an organization changes, and it may begin to work differently or work for a different purpose. The leader is responsible for keeping the congregation informed of the goals he is seeking to reach. He should ask congregational approval when changes are made.

In addition to goals, the program leader should recommend to the church the activities of the program for each year. These activities should lead directly and positively toward the goals of the program. The activities should produce desirable results for the church. Co-ordination of activities should be accomplished through the church council.

Organizations usually carry on more work than is imme-

diately apparent by their name. For example, the Sunday school is much more than a school. In chapter 4 you will see that its tasks include other work which the church needs to do. This work should not be thought of as just the work of the Sunday school organization. It should be seen as the work which the Sunday school does for the church. A program of visitation sponsored by the Sunday school should be a church program of visitation. Many times pastors and Sunday school leaders complain that the people do not support the visitation program. Perhaps it is because the people have not really established a church visitation program.

After careful evaluation and understanding of the need a program meets, congregational approval of a program should be congregational consent to support and participate in that program.

When leaders begin to involve the congregation in decisions about planned future action, they are working according to democratic processes. In addition, leaders set forward their own work in that the congregation participates more intelligently in this particular area of church life and commits itself to a better support of the work. The leader's recommendations should not include every detail he is planning. Neither should the leader withhold information so that the church does not fully comprehend his recommendation or see it in relation to the purposes and objectives of the congregation.

3. *Report*

The church provides resources for the programs it establishes. The organizations are provided leaders from the congregation. They are provided finances to purchase equipment and supplies, and to support activities. Buildings are erected and maintained in order that programs may be carried on. Therefore, the program leader has the responsibility to account to the congregation for the proper use of the resources provided. Some leaders never consider the large amount of personal time, dollars, and building investment which have been entrusted to them and their organization by

the congregation. A proper understanding of these facts should convince any program leader of the trust the congregation has in him. He should also realize his serious responsibility for reporting actions and decisions to the congregation or for requesting the congregation to take action. In accepting such reports, the congregation is relieving him and his co-workers of purely personal responsibility. They assume a share of the success or failure of any venture which they approve. Hearing a report of the work of an organization is also a way in which the congregation can review the work of God.

Leaders should report to the congregation the achievements in their area of responsibility. Since the congregation has delegated a specific responsibility to a leader and has provided him with helpers, finances, and a place to work, the congregation has a right to know what has been accomplished.

IV. LEGAL AND FORMAL MEANS FOR CONDUCTING CHURCH AFFAIRS

As congregations increase in size and complexity, many things which were once taken for granted need to be stated formally. Such action provides a safeguard to the congregation, its officers, and the witness of Christ in the community.

1. *Church Constitution*

A constitution is the congregation's formal statement of what it is and how it operates. Such a statement is needed to give direction to the officers of the church and to the members in carrying on the work of the church. The constitution should reflect the democratic processes which the congregation wishes to use in conducting its affairs. Allen W. Graves has said, "The constitution should set forth the basic principles governing the church, and the bylaws should describe how the church organization is to function." [2] Some

---

[2] Allen W. Graves, "Has Your Church Considered the Advantages of a Constitution and Bylaws?," *Church Administration,* III (October, 1961), 15.

churches may desire to include a doctrinal statement in their constitutions. In so doing, they set a standard by which the work of the church may be measured.

A constitution should be more than a formal statement filed among the records of the church. It, in addition to the New Testament, should be the standard by which the congregation measures itself. The constitution needs to include the name of the church, its location, a statement of purpose and objectives, the nature and requirements for membership, offices and the method of electing officers, meetings, financial policy, ordinances, established church organizations, policies concerning church property and other legal matters, basis of co-operation with other Baptist churches, and the quorum necessary to do church business. Bylaws may include additional information, such as procedures for carrying out various activities of the church, policies regarding the use of buildings or equipment, and other information needed by church members and those who do business with the church.

2. *Church Business Meeting*

Perhaps the most misunderstood and misused meeting of the congregation is the business meeting. This should be the time when the congregation determines its course of action; authorizes the use of its resources of leadership, finances, and buildings; hears the report of its leaders; evaluates the actions and results of the congregation's work; and expresses freely the viewpoints and desires of the individual members. When properly understood and planned, the church business meeting should be a time to review the work of God and to give thanksgiving for his accomplishments.

If democratic processes are followed, the congregation will be informed well ahead of time about matters to be discussed. Full information should be shared. Truth, the whole truth, is the only basis for congregational action. If information is lacking or if unanswerable questions are raised, action should be delayed. Reports by program leaders should include more than mere statistics. The congregation

should be furnished information that will help it evaluate its work. The church business meeting, even more than the Sunday morning worship hour, could bring the congregation to one mind and one accord. Whether this goal is accomplished will depend upon what the church business meeting is planned to do.

The moderator and clerk are two officers of the church who are essential in conducting the church business meeting. It is the task of the moderator to guide the discussions of the congregation and to keep the business meeting running smoothly toward its desired goals. The effective moderator will be well acquainted with parliamentary law, the constitution and bylaws of his church, principles of group discussion, and the purpose or purposes of each business meeting. He will refrain from constant participation in the discussion of the congregation. He must learn especially how to allow persons to disagree with the church program or to express emotions freely. He must be able to respond in a Christian manner toward such persons and even to help them express themselves so that they do not feel rejected. Free, even emotional, expression is the right of every person in a democracy. The office of moderator exists to assure each member this privilege.

The church clerk is responsible for maintaining a record of the actions of the congregation. In the minutes he prepares, he should accurately represent the actions of the congregation and the expressions of the members. Minutes should not include unimportant facts or the clerk's personal viewpoint. A record of exactly what happened should be stated in a manner that can be understood by those who read it decades later. In addition to recording the minutes of church business meetings, the clerk is also responsible for maintaining official correspondence for the congregation, church records, and records of the membership roll, and for preparing the associational report.

3. *Trustees*

Many congregations have established the office of trustee

for overseeing legal matters for the church. If the church owns property and is not incorporated, the legal titles must be conveyed to trustees who represent the congregation. The office of trustee is established because of the relationship of the church to the civil government. Porter W. Routh points out the relationship of the trustee to the congregation: "That a trustee cannot act on his own initiative or on his own behalf should be clearly understood. A trustee is selected by vote of confidence of the body which selects him, and the law demands perfect faith and integrity of the trustee and the discharge of his obligation." [3]

The selection of trustees by a congregation is a witness to the community that it plans to conduct its outside business affairs in the same dependable, faithful, and honest manner in which the congregation expects each of its members to act.

4. *The Church Council*

One of the most important but often neglected groups in the church is the church council. The council is responsible for planning, co-ordinating, and evaluating the various programs of the church. A church that feels fragmented, fails to set objectives, misuses time, and duplicates efforts usually does not have a properly functioning church council. The council should not interpose itself between the congregation and the officers elected to report directly to the congregation. Rather, its attention should be directed to co-ordinating the programs of the church into one program.

The church council furnishes a means by which the program leaders can relate their actions and the actions of their organizations to the main thrust of the church program. Through the council they share information with one another. Planning is based on the idea of giving priority to the most significant and essential activities of the church. The church calendar and the congregation's time are properly considered. This eliminates useless meetings. Meetings

---

[3] Porter W. Routh, "What Is a Trustee?," *Church Administration,* II (December, 1960), 24.

and activities with purpose will be properly scheduled. Personal conflicts and organizational rivalries can be solved by the leaders on the basis of what is best for the church. Time and energy of the congregation and pastor will be conserved through the meeting of the council. Church leaders, such as the Sunday school superintendent, Training Union director, Woman's Missionary Union president, Brotherhood president, or the treasurer will learn to make decisions in light of what is best for the church. As the council evaluates the work that is being done by the organizations represented, several questions should be kept constantly before it:

Are our actions related to God's will for our church as we understand the objectives set by our congregation?

Are we doing what is most important at the proper time, and are we making the best use of the proper resources?

Are our programs being carried out on a sound basis, or do we lead haphazardly?

Are the results of our work evident?

Are the members of the congregation becoming more deeply involved in the significant activities of our church?

Are we acting in democratic fashion by identifying the decisions which should be made by the congregation and by providing proper information to the congregation for making these decisions?

Are we taking the initiative delegated to us in bringing to the attention of the congregation new and better ways to accomplish the basic functions for which the church exists?

The church council is a necessity to the church that believes in congregational government and is trying to carry on multiple programs. It is the church's instrument for eliminating duplication, inefficiency, confusion, and fragmentation.

5. *Organizations and Officers*

Most church members do not realize how many major continuing activities their congregation is carrying on. This is because the church has assigned many tasks to each organization. Sunday school, for example, does much more than teach the biblical revelation for the church. The follow-

The Task of Church Leaders

ing organizations carry out educational and other tasks for the church: Sunday school, Training Union, Music Ministry, Woman's Missionary Union, and Brotherhood.

A church educational organization is a structured approach to learning. Such an organization has a philosophy, objectives, programed learning activities, and leaders to conduct these activities. It has a clearly defined constituency and content areas which are properly related to those of other church educational organizations.

A church educational organization maintains a regular schedule of meetings for learning consistent with the best educational principles and methods. It provides planned curriculum materials and activities designed to accomplish its objectives.

In addition to these program organizations, the church may establish program services and committees such as the audio-visual aids, recreation, finance, or personnel to be responsible for program or administrative services. Some responsibilities may be delegated to officers such as the church moderator, clerk, treasurer, or trustees.

V. Recommending and Reporting to the Congregation

When the congregation has provided its leaders with formal means for carrying on their work, these leaders are ready to fulfil their responsibilities to the congregation. These responsibilities are fulfilled normally by recommending and reporting. Church leaders should recommend regularly for congregational approval changes and improvement in objectives, programs, activities, and the use of resources.

Reports to the congregation should be well planned. They should be stated in terms of the objectives of the church. If the church has not yet stated its objectives, then a leader should state the accomplishments in terms of the objectives established for his own area of responsibility.

Church leaders have the opportunity of leading the congregation to understand the meaning of its existence. They can assist the congregation in becoming the body of Christ,

CHAPTER 4

I. TEACH THE BIBLICAL REVELATION

   1. Nature of the Biblical Revelation
   2. Content of the Biblical Revelation
   3. Purpose of the Biblical Revelation

II. REACH ALL PROSPECTS FOR THE CHURCH

   1. Outreach, a Basic Characteristic of a Church
   2. Sunday School Best Suited for Task

III. LEAD ALL CHURCH MEMBERS TO WITNESS DAILY

   1. Meaning of Witnessing
   2. Witnessing, the Responsibility of Every Christian
   3. Taking Advantage of Witnessing Opportunities
   4. Sunday School, the Logical Organization for Encouraging Witnessing

IV. LEAD ALL CHURCH MEMBERS TO WORSHIP DAILY

V. PROVIDE OPPORTUNITIES FOR THE PERSONAL MINISTRIES OF THE CHURCH

   1. The Need for Personal Ministries
   2. Christ, the Example to Follow
   3. Sunday School Responsible for Conducting the Program of Personal Ministries

VI. PROVIDE ORGANIZATION AND LEADERSHIP FOR SPECIAL PROJECTS OF THE CHURCH

   1. Revival Meetings
   2. Church Budget Campaigns
   3. Special Missions Offerings

VII. PROVIDE AND INTERPRET INFORMATION REGARDING THE WORK OF THE CHURCH AND THE DENOMINATION

4

The Task of
THE SUNDAY SCHOOL

IF A CHURCH is to be a church, its basic actions must be identified, stated, planned, and conducted. Unless these essential steps are taken, a church will find itself engaged in "busyness" instead of being about the Master's business.

Already we have noted that education is a function of the church. Involving church members in learning is so necessary that a church cannot fully be a church if it fails to educate its members. Southern Baptist churches give strong emphasis to their function of education. They have developed educational organizations according to the pattern defined in chapter 3. They have entrusted to them much of the learning activities for their constituencies.

In addition, Southern Baptist churches have assigned to their organizations major tasks which are related to their educational responsibilities. Such assignment gives each organization significant church tasks to perform and makes the organization essential to the work of the churches.

In this chapter and in subsequent ones, the tasks of the various church educational organizations will be discussed. In each instance the study programs of the organization will be considered. In addition, the related tasks which have been either assigned by the church or developed through utilization by the church will be studied.

The organization carrying the heaviest responsibilities is

the Sunday school. It is ideally suited for this position of trust. Most Southern Baptist churches have Sunday schools, and their combined enrolment is the largest Sunday school membership in the world. The Sunday school is a permanent organization meeting each Sunday and conducting its work regularly each week. Its workers are among the most faithful, loyal, and dedicated members of the church. The textbook of the Sunday school is the Bible, which is foundational to all other study materials in church educational programs.

The Vacation Bible school and Weekday Bible Study programs are phases of Sunday school work which enhance and enlarge the ongoing Bible-teaching program of the church.

Consideration will begin with a study of the principal tasks of the Sunday school.

I. TEACH THE BIBLICAL REVELATION

The Bible has been the textbook of the Sunday school from the first development of lesson courses to the present. But there are many ways to study the Bible. In the Sunday school one may begin with Genesis and study the Bible book by book. If such study were conducted according to this pattern, a child would reach voting age before beginning his study of Matthew. The Bible may also be studied according to classifications such as history, poetry, and the Gospels. It may be studied biographically or according to periods of history.

However, the most effective approach to Bible study is teaching the biblical revelation. What is meant by the biblical revelation? "Revelation in the Christian sense is that self-disclosure of God in Christ which makes it possible for man to know God and to live a life of fellowship with him." [1] "The record of this revelation—the literary means of its transmission to us—is the Bible. Revelation produced the Bible." [2]

Reaching persons for Bible study is the basic task of the

---

[1] W. T. Conner, *Christian Doctrine* (Nashville: Broadman Press, 1937), p. 27.

[2] *Ibid.*, p. 35.

Sunday school. It is impossible to teach unless there is someone to learn. The minimum requirement of a teaching situation is something to teach, a teacher, a learner, and effective communication between the two.

Yet, the importance of the message to be learned is the reason for reaching people to learn it. Therefore, we start the discussion of the task of the Sunday school with a consideration of what the Sunday school is to teach. For years emphasis in the Sunday school has been on the study of the Bible. It is the value and importance of the content of the Bible which should motivate each Sunday school worker to reach people to study it.

As scriptural authority for reaching people we often quote Luke 14 : 23—"The lord said unto the servant, Go out into the highways and hedges, and compel them to come in, that my house may be filled"—without studying the preceding verses. The marriage feast had already been prepared, and the guests who were invited failed to come. For that reason, the servants were told to find other guests. The prepared feast was the reason for inviting guests. Reaching individuals is the responsibility of every Sunday school, but individuals are to be reached for Bible study. Before going after prospects, a Sunday school should make certain that every person invited to attend will be spiritually fed if he comes.

Since what is to be studied in the Sunday school is so important, let us examine further what is meant by the biblical revelation.

1. *Nature of the Biblical Revelation*

The biblical revelation began in the heart and mind of God. The Bible is the record of the revelation of God and is, at the same time, the revelation of God. It is his inspired word. His disclosure is evident in divine intervention in the affairs of men, in historical acts and events, and in the divinely inspired interpretations of these interventions.

Jesus Christ is the climactic center and key to the meaning of the biblical revelation. The full and ultimate disclosure of God's being came through his Son.

Both the Old and New Testaments are essential to understanding the biblical revelation. The New Testament records the fulfilment of the Old, and full understanding of the New Testament is incomplete without the Old. The full meaning of the Old is understandable only as interpreted in the light of the New. The two compose a co-ordinated unity.

The Bible, as a record of God's self-disclosure, is a God-given revelation. It is divinely inspired. Other than ordinary processes account for its existence. Both divine and human factors were involved in its production. God breathed upon men to bring into being the inspired scriptural writings. He directed the preservation of the scriptural writings and their selection to be included in the Bible. The Scriptures both compose and record God's revelations.

2. *Content of the Biblical Revelation*

God's initial manifestations of himself came in creation. The full sweep of creation indicates his authorship of all life. Creation made evident the designing nature of God's being. God's control over his creation is maintained through the order of his creation. God limited his control when he created man in his own image and gave him freedom of will.

Man is the object of God's self-disclosure. Man was created so that he might respond to God. Man is a person; his being is eternal.

The climax of God's self-disclosure came in Christ, who revealed God's nature, being, and purpose for man. In Christ, God demonstrated the life toward which redeemed man is to strive. In God's disclosure in Christ he established the heart of history.

The biblical revelation indicates a God-directed plan for his people to compose a fellowship of followers. This plan is fully expressed in the church. Jesus Christ brought the church into being during his earthly ministry. Its nature, purpose, and functions progressively unfold in the New Testament writing. The church is a fellowship of the redeemed children of God.

God included in his self-disclosure the revelation of the person and work of the Holy Spirit. Throughout the Old Testament the nature and work of the Spirit is evidenced, but only in the New Testament are his person and ministry fully revealed. The Spirit came in power at Pentecost following Jesus' ascension. The Holy Spirit is the revealing agent for understanding the nature and meaning of God's self-revelation and his will for man.

God's self-disclosure points toward a consummation of all things. Creation awaits ultimate redemption. God's people await ultimate redemption. They are to experience complete liberation from the limitations of earthly existence in the complete freedom of fellowship with, and service to, the Redeemer. Consummation necessitates a final judgment. God is judge as well as Father. This judgment will banish all that is superficial.

3. *Purpose of the Biblical Revelation*

The purpose of the biblical revelation is to bring man into a living relationship with God through faith in Jesus Christ. Within this relationship man will fulfil God's unique and creative purpose for him. This purpose is significantly reflected in the biblical revelation. It speaks to the totality of man. It interprets the meaning of life and its context. It identifies man's being in relation to God. The revelation provides redeemed man with the needed guiding principles for redeemed living.

The Sunday school has been entrusted with teaching the record of God's self-disclosure to man. This purpose gives tremendous significance to the teacher and his preparation. It also gives great significance to every class session, as a teacher seeks to lead his class members to understand God's self-disclosure and his reasons for revealing himself to man. It is such understandings as these which add meaning not only to the Sunday school task of teaching the biblical revelation but also to its task of outreach.

II. Reach All Prospects for the Church

Reaching prospects is maintaining personal contact with every unsaved and unenrolled person in the community so as to establish a relationship with him for Christ and the church. The major purpose of outreach is to bring each prospect under the influence of the gospel through faithfully attending the regular meetings of the educational organizations and the worship services of the church. Through outreach it is hoped that each unsaved person will be won to Christ and will be led to place his membership in a church, to participate in the programs of the church educational organizations, and to engage in Christian service as a faithful church member.

Reaching out to enrol all unenlisted persons for Bible study is basic if persons are to be reached permanently for the churches. If the prospects can attend, they should be enrolled in the departments which meet on Sunday. If they cannot attend regularly, they should be enrolled in the Extension department.

In the Extension department they may be visited regularly by department visitors. Those in rest homes, hospitals, business institutions, jails, and penitentiaries may be taught through extension Bible classes conducted for them at convenient times by Extension department workers.

But reaching all prospects means more than enrolling and and teaching individuals in classes. Reaching in the sense used here means that each prospect is being visited regularly for the church by some member of the Sunday school. Although the Sunday school member desires for him to be in Sunday school and is working to that end, the main purpose is to meet the personal needs of the prospect where he is until he is led to attend and participate. Teaching in this sense will be done in homes and in places of business, according to the informal teaching opportunities which develop during visits. Such teaching can be done best through conversation in which Scripture passages appropriate to the needs and problems of each person are used at the most opportune times. Through regular visitation each prospect can

be properly related to a church. Such personal contacts may need to be maintained over the years, even though a person never attends on Sunday.

1. *Outreach, a Basic Characteristic of a Church*

Concern for the unreached is one of the basic characteristics of a church. If a church does not have this concern, it is more a social club than a church. Of course, every church must be concerned about the members already enlisted— whether they are growing, developing, and maturing as church members. If a church becomes wholly introspective, however, it tends to become self-centered and self-satisfied. The result is a dying church. Some members of almost every church are looking for a place to stop church activities. They even talk of buying the last piece of property and constructing the last building. This they often do in the midst of unlimited prospects at their doors, or immediately beyond, and with millions of lost people in distant lands.

It would be a new concept for many churches if they were to realize that they cannot bring all of their prospects to their buildings. Not all of their prospects will respond to visits. Church members must take their church to the prospects. This is the reason why missions must be established, perhaps only one to three blocks away from the church itself. This is why new churches must be started across the river, the highway, the railroad—wherever there are people to be reached.

Baptists have learned how to multiply units of organization within a church and thereby reach more people. We have yet to learn how to multiply churches by encouraging groups of members to establish other churches and missions. Churches in pioneer Southern Baptist areas often put to shame older, established churches by the number of new missions and churches they have started. Whenever a church becomes satisfied with the number of members it has and is not concerned with reaching people with the gospel, it is not fulfilling its function as a church.

Jesus said, "As my Father hath sent me, even so send I

you" (John 20:21). He also said to his disciples, "Pray ye therefore the Lord of the harvest, that he will send forth labourers into his harvest" (Matt. 9:38). As a final commission, Jesus said to his followers, "Go ye therefore, and teach all nations, baptizing them in the name of the Father, and of the Son, and of the Holy Ghost" (Matt. 28:19). These and many other of Jesus' commands indicate that a church ought always to have compassion and concern for those who are not being reached.

2. *Sunday School Best Suited for Task*

Baptist churches in the twentieth century need a strategy for accomplishing their tasks. Their best strategy lies in the use of their educational organizations. If the churches do not use these organizations, they will have to develop other organizations or strategy. It is only logical to use what is already available.

The Sunday school is unlike other schools. Teachers and pupils in the Sunday school are responsible for recruiting members for their classes. The church can use this principle as its strategy for accomplishing its task of outreach. Thus the outreach of the church can be handled successfully by the Sunday school. This means that the church program of visitation for prospects should be conducted by the Sunday school. The Sunday school developed the religious census as a basic instrument for locating prospects. It developed a plan for enlargement designed to increase the membership of Sunday school classes and departments. The provision of adequate space and the development of a continuous visitation plan are other factors in Sunday school enlargement. All of these fundamentals of Sunday school enlargement make the Sunday school ideally suited for use by the church in reaching prospects.

III. Lead All Church Members to Witness Daily

Outreach and witness are responsibilities which are basic to the effective functioning of every church. These actions determine the evangelistic thrust of each congregation. Just

as every church member is needed to find prospects, so every church member is needed to witness daily.

1. *Meaning of Witnessing*

"Witness" is a term used by Jesus: "But ye shall receive power, after that the Holy Ghost is come upon you: and ye shall be witnesses unto me both in Jerusalem, and in all Judea, and in Samaria, and unto the uttermost part of the earth" (Acts 1:8). The word "martyr" is from the Greek and means witness. This word came to indicate a person who sealed his testimony with his blood.

Christians in every generation should share with others what God through Christ has done for them. This witness should be to the unsaved persons with whom one has contact. Every church member should be constantly alert to his opportunities to share with such persons what God through Christ means to him. In this way every Christian would become an evangelist and would share in the evangelistic task of his church.

But Christians should witness also to each other. Christians should bear testimony to their fellow Christians regarding the blessings of God which they have experienced. In the church prayer meeting of another generation this kind of witnessing was done regularly. Little opportunity is afforded in present-day church life, however, for this type of spiritual experience. This lack may explain in part the various types of prayer retreats and cell groups which are becoming increasingly popular. When church members share their spiritual experiences with each other, their faith is strengthened. This type of conversation is needed as Christian friends talk together wherever or whenever they get together, either in person or by telephone.

By giving money through the church budget, a person can witness through those who serve as missionaries. Money used for missions extends the witness of each Christian.

2. *Witnessing, the Responsibility of Every Christian*

According to many church members, the pastor is paid to

witness for the church. In keeping with such a concept, it is little wonder that this saying has developed: "The pastor is paid to be good, but the layman is good for nothing." Where is there a pastor who has not been asked by his members to witness to unsaved persons?

Perhaps a larger group of church members feel that witnessing is the responsibility of the pastor, the employed staff of the church, the deacons, and the Sunday school officers and teachers. When these workers were selected, the church members who approved them happily voted for them to do the evangelistic work of the church.

Such concepts cannot be justified by the New Testament. Witnessing is the responsibility of every Christian. Until a church deliberately sets itself to lead every member of the church to witness, it is failing as a New Testament church.

3. *Taking Advantage of Witnessing Opportunities*

Every church member should witness daily. Opportunities for witnessing start the moment one awakens in the morning. The manner in which he greets other members of his family is a way of witnessing. One may witness also by the way he drives to work.

If each church member drove his car as he should, traffic fatalities would drop, and there would be a Christian witness on the streets and highways, where, perhaps, it is needed more greatly than anywhere else. It is amazing how Christian courtesy and consideration vanish when a person is behind the steering wheel of his car.

Many a Christian who faces opportunities each day to witness never witnesses. This same Christian may go to his church at night, engage in the visitation of prospects, and contact fewer of them than he could have contacted all day at his work. Many churches worry about their territory. In witnessing, a church's territory may be defined by the activities of its members. The territory of a church extends wherever its members are serving and witnessing at any given moment.

We must get back to the New Testament concept that wit-

nessing begins when we awaken in the morning and continues throughout our waking hours. We should be sensitive and alert to every opportunity to witness for Christ, whether to the saved or unsaved. A positive Christian testimony is needed in every area of life every day. Until we accept our responsibility, Christianity will never be the world movement Christ intended it to be.

4. *Sunday School, the Logical Organization for Encouraging Witnessing.*

The church as the body of Christ has many activities. The Sunday school is a part of this functioning body. When the Sunday school works, it is the church in action. It has unsaved members already enrolled in its classes. It engages in the task of reaching all prospects for the church. Therefore, the Sunday school is the logical organization of the church to lead church members to witness daily. It can give each church member an opportunity to express himself in dynamic Christian faith and action. The enlistment of every church member in witnessing can become the church's thrust into the unregenerate community in which it is located. The Training Union can join the Sunday school in this endeavor by training church members how to witness daily.

IV. LEAD ALL CHURCH MEMBERS TO WORSHIP DAILY

No other experience of a church member is as important as worship. God created man with the ability to worship so that he and man could have fellowship together. God is always ready to engage in this fellowship, but man is so self-centered and preoccupied that often he denies himself this spiritual experience.

A church must provide worship opportunities for its members and lead them to draw near to God each day. One of the best ways to do this is to provide for worship experiences in the church building. The pastor, staff members, and deacons should plan for experiences of worship in the church worship services. All parts of a worship service

should be related properly so that they will contribute to the worship experiences of the members.

The regular and faithful attendance of church members must be maintained if they are to become involved in worship opportunities. The task of making this attendance possible is readily accepted by the Sunday school. A visit to reach people should include an invitation to attend the church worship services. When a member or visitor attends Sunday school, he should be invited to remain for the morning worship service. The relationship between inviting persons to attend both Sunday school and the worship services is one of the principal reasons for having the Sunday school prior to the worship service each Sunday morning.

Not only should the Sunday school lead members to attend the church worship services; it should lead them to worship. It can make this contribution by planning for worship experiences in Sunday school. Assembly programs offer excellent potentialities for worship. If planned properly, these programs can provide the atmosphere, graded materials, planned experiences, and dedicated leadership conducive to a genuine experience of worship.

However, the Sunday school's greatest opportunity to lead church members to worship daily comes as the worship experiences on Sunday are carried over into the activities of the week. Since the Sunday school has the Bible as its textbook, it is logical that each member should have his own Bible and read it daily. The study of the biblical materials outlined in the lesson courses is important. Each church member should engage in the daily reading of devotional passages in the Bible which will lead him to worship. This he may do privately or as a member of his family.

Families, as units of the church, should be encouraged to worship daily at a scheduled time. Parents should prepare for worship opportunities by using the available materials that are geared to helping them lead in the worship periods.

When a person reads the Bible, God speaks to him through his Word. As God speaks, it is natural to respond.

Soon prayer is a part of the experience. As each church member reads his Bible and prays daily, he will outgrow selfish praying and enlarge the circumference of his prayer life.

This is the reason that names of missionaries are listed with Bible readings.

As the Sunday school leads each church member to worship daily, the Training Union teaches and trains church members in the art of worship. Special materials are provided for this purpose so that these two organizations may work together in making worship central in the experiences of church members.

As a part of its church task of leading members to worship, the Sunday school will work with the Training Union, Woman's Missionary Union, and the Brotherhood in leading all church members to attend the Sunday evening and midweek prayer services of their churches. These additional worship opportunities are neglected by many church members. As the Sunday school lends this support to the Sunday evening services of the church, it will lead increasing numbers of church members to use Sunday evening for fellowship with God.

V. Provide Opportunities for the Personal Ministries of the Church

In addition to the tasks of outreach, witnessing, and worship, another task of the Sunday school is to provide opportunities for the personal ministries of a church. A new concept of the value of the person is needed by every church member. A person is a total personality—body, intellect, and spirit.

1. *The Need for Personal Ministries*

Each church needs to take a fresh look at its function of ministry. At present, the Nursery department seems to have the most effective ministry to the total person. Workers in this department attempt to meet the physical and emotional needs of each baby. At the same time, they attempt to lay

the foundation for guiding his learning experiences and developing his spiritual life. However, as soon as the young child learns to take care of his bodily needs, his physical nature seems to be forgotten. From this time on, aside from occasional parties, banquets, and similar activities, little is done to meet his physical and societal needs.

Even when trying to meet the pressing needs of hungry persons in our community, we limit our personal ministries largely to Thanksgiving and Christmas. It is unfortunate that these two holidays come so close together. If Thanksgiving were in July rather than in November, those we remember would benefit more from our gifts. What is being done by churches to meet the total needs of persons? What should be done in order to minister adequately to these needs?

2. *Christ, the Example to Follow*

The ministry of Christ abounds with examples of his concern for the physical needs of persons. He healed lepers, gave sight to the blind, cast out demons, and raised Lazarus from the dead.

As previously indicated, one of the best condensed statements of Christ's concern for the physical needs of persons is found in Matthew 25 : 35–36: "For I was an hungred, and ye gave me meat: I was thirsty, and ye gave me drink: I was a stranger, and ye took me in: naked, and ye clothed me: I was sick, and ye visited me: I was in prison, and ye came unto me." In ministering to personal needs, one ministers to Christ.

3. *Sunday School Responsible for Conducting the Program of Personal Ministries*

It should be repeated that the teaching task of the Sunday school is its most important task. Teaching the biblical revelation is the Sunday school's major responsibility; its other tasks grow out of it.

Church members through outreach and witnessing will discover many persons with varying needs. They should

endeavor to meet these needs in the spirit of Christ. Such persons need someone to understand them, love them, and express compassion and concern for them. Some are members of a church; others are not. The church exists to meet the needs of all persons.

A church should have a well-developed, well-administered program of personal ministries. It must be a church program, but the Sunday school should have the responsibility for conducting it.

VI. PROVIDE ORGANIZATION AND LEADERSHIP FOR SPECIAL PROJECTS OF THE CHURCH

Because of the nature, purpose, and functions of the Sunday school, it is usable in conducting special projects which are related to its Bible-teaching ministry.

A project is an activity which can be conducted in a brief period of time, such as a few days or a few weeks.

1. *Revival Meetings*

It has been found that the Sunday school is the church's most valuable agency for use preceding, during, and following revival meetings. The Sunday school may be used to take a census prior to a revival meeting. With the census returns in hand, the leaders of the Sunday school can tabulate the evangelistic prospects of the church. These include not only persons found in the census but also unsaved and unenlisted Sunday school members. Sunday school prospects will include the unsaved and unenlisted parents of Sunday school members.

During the revival, the Sunday school should lead all church members to witness and to invite all prospects to attend.

Special department decision services may be conducted on Sunday morning during the revival, which will give opportunities for persons to accept Christ. Some churches conduct special services for the entire Sunday school during revival meetings.

The Sunday school is also helpful in the follow-up of revivals. New converts may be assigned to the Sunday school for visitation and enlistment. The concern of Sunday school workers for the unsaved by no means stops at baptism. The new convert must be instructed in the Christian life. This instruction is carried out best through the Sunday school. Bible study, the life-long need of every church member, should be recognized as such not only by the church but also by individual church members.

Another task of the Sunday school is to enlist all new church members in other church organizations and in the total life and work of the church. This is another way the Sunday school may contribute to the development of the new church member and to the growth of other church organizations.

2. *Church Budget Campaigns*

The Sunday school has become the church's chief instrument in the subscription and payment of church budgets. It is impossible to teach the biblical revelation without teaching stewardship. Such teaching requires time and must cover the basic principles of stewardship necessary for a person to become a faithful steward of his possessions. A Christian must grow spiritually in order to become a good steward. On the other hand, a person will grow spiritually as he gives.

The Sunday school is useful in making preparation for a church budget campaign. Opportunity is provided to members to sign pledge cards in their departments or classes. Here a teacher has the advantage of encouraging personal participation because of his contacts with his pupils. His request for his class member to sign a pledge card is a way of teaching the stewardship of money. Learning should issue in practice. Therefore, what a person learns regarding the stewardship of money should be expressed in making a pledge to the church budget. Making a pledge will also assist him in learning how to give.

The Sunday school teacher is also the best person for the

task of obtaining pledges from Sunday school members who are absent on pledge day. Teachers should visit their class members regularly. When this practice is followed, the teacher's visit to obtain a pledge is normal procedure. The Sunday school is also useful in calling to the attention of each church member the need for a weekly payment in keeping with his pledge. By providing offering envelopes to be used each Sunday, the Sunday school emphasizes the values of a budget system.

3. *Special Missions Offerings*

In 20 per cent of Southern Baptist churches, the Sunday school is the only church educational organization. For this reason, the Sunday school is used for special missions days and offerings. Home Missions Day in the Sunday school and Foreign Missions Day in the Sunday school now follow the Home Missions and Foreign Missions weeks of prayer in the denominational calendar. The Sunday School Department of the Sunday School Board co-operates with the two mission boards and with Woman's Missionary Union and the Brotherhood in presenting annually these two missions causes. Sunday schools also present state missions, at which time special offerings are received in many states.

Of particular assistance to the churches in evangelism, stewardship, and missions is the Vacation Bible school. It is one of the most valuable agents the church has for winning children and youth to Christ. The number who are won to Christ and who make life committments each year is increasing. The Vacation Bible school also gives major emphasis to the Cooperative Program and the various objects included in it. The offerings received in the worship periods each year go to the Cooperative Program. These offerings increase from year to year, but the most valuable contribution is stewardship education. Educating Vacation Bible school members in the needs of denominational causes strengthens the future program of Southern Baptist churches.

VII. PROVIDE AND INTERPRET INFORMATION REGARDING
THE WORK OF THE CHURCH AND THE DENOMINATION

In addition to its major task of Bible teaching, the
Sunday school is a great informational agency. Arthur Flake,
in *The True Functions of the Sunday School,* declared this
to be a task of the Sunday school.

In each church, the Sunday school can be an informational agency for church events and emphases. Workers in
the Sunday school can keep before their members the major
tasks which are being undertaken by the church. This
information may be interpreted by the pastor, staff members, or general superintendent in the weekly officers and
teachers' meeting or in the monthly officers' council. Such
information may then be taken by department superintendents, other officers, and teachers to departments and
classes the following Sunday. Care must be taken not to
make department and class sessions purely promotional
in nature. Only activities and emphases with major significance to the church should be brought to the attention
of Sunday school members. The teaching period should be
protected at all costs. The Sunday school can disseminate
both church and denominational information in such a way
as to unify the entire Sunday school program and properly
relate it to the church and through the church to the denomination.

The Sunday School Department of the Sunday School
Board is a channel department. As a channel department,
it not only develops a total program of Sunday school
work but also provides a channel by which other programs
of the Sunday School Board and the denomination are
carried to the churches.

In long-range planning, the Sunday School Department
of the Sunday School Board relates to the other boards,
agencies, and institutions of the Southern Baptist Convention when their programs are relevant to its program.

The Sunday School Builder carries articles each month on
emphases in the denominational calendar. This magazine

makes it possible for every Sunday school member to know what his denomination is emphasizing each month in the year. With a large constituency and with a Sunday school in almost every church, the Sunday school can become Southern Baptists' greatest informational agency.

CHAPTER 5

I. INTERPRET SYSTEMATIC THEOLOGY, CHRISTIAN ETHICS, CHRISTIAN HISTORY, AND CHURCH POLITY AND ORGANIZATION
1. Interpret Systematic Theology
2. Interpret Christian Ethics
3. Interpret Christian History
4. Interpret Church Polity and Organization

II. GIVE ORIENTATION TO NEW CHURCH MEMBERS
1. Objectives
2. Scope

III. TRAIN CHURCH MEMBERS TO PERFORM THE FUNCTIONS OF THEIR CHURCH

IV. DISCOVER, RECRUIT, AND GIVE GENERAL TRAINING TO POTENTIAL LEADERS OF THE CHURCH
1. Discover Potential Leaders
2. Recruit Potential Leaders
3. Train Potential Leaders

V. PROVIDE ORGANIZATION AND LEADERSHIP FOR SPECIAL PROJECTS OF THE CHURCH

VI. PROVIDE AND INTERPRET INFORMATION REGARDING THE WORK OF THE CHURCH AND THE DENOMINATION

5

The Task of

THE TRAINING UNION

THE TRAINING UNION is the second largest educational organization in Southern Baptist churches. It is distinctive in that it trains church members to perform their full responsibilities as members of their congregations. It has the responsibility of training all church members and giving general training to potential leaders of the church. No other denomination has an organization similar to the Training Union. Because Southern Baptist churches have it, they can provide greater study opportunities for their members and have added assistance in achieving their tasks.

We have noted that the Sunday school teaches the biblical revelation and is concerned with leading persons to saving faith in Jesus Christ, to membership in a Baptist church, and to growth in the Christian faith and life. Because of these concerns, the Sunday school has an unlimited constituency. It teaches both the saved and the unsaved, the church member and the non-church member, the youngest baby and the oldest adult.

The Training Union, although vitally concerned with evangelism and the growth of Christians, seeks to enrol church members and their children for learning. It trains church members to work together within the fellowship of a church and to be effective church members wherever they go. Its primary concern is training church members to per-

form the functions of their churches. The Training Union succeeds best when all church organizations grow, when the church is strengthened, and when individuals are trained to become responsible church members.

Southern Baptist churches are now utilizing their Training Unions to a greater extent than ever before. The Training Union began as a young people's movement. Only in recent years have churches given significant attention to the selection and training of leaders for this organization.

The Sunday school works with each individual, seeking to lead him to commit his will and purpose to Christ and to become an active member of a church. The Training Union works with each individual as a church member—a member of a functioning fellowship.

It is difficult to find a clear-cut illustration of the preceding statement. Perhaps an example from the sports world may throw further light on this difference. A track coach may have a brilliant sprinter whose specialty is the one-hundred-yard dash. The coach may develop this athlete to the extent that he wins a number of events in track meets.

In the fall this same sprinter may come out for the football team. The sprinting ability which he developed under the track coach will serve him well as an end on the football team. However, he has many additional tasks to learn as a member of a team. He must learn to master the signals, to follow the leadership of his quarterback, to receive passes, and to do other tasks required of him. All this he must do in co-operation with ten other men as his teammates. The football coach is no less concerned with him as an individual than is the track coach. He is more concerned, however, with training him to win at football by being a member of the team.

Anyone who has ever sat through a church business meeting knows what it would mean if every church member could play on the same team just once. If football teams were like some Baptist churches, the ball carrier would be tackled behind his own line by his teammates. A Baptist deacon is quoted as having said that as long as he was a

member of his church, it would never have a unanimous vote. Such a man needs to join the team.

The Sunday school develops persons in the Christian life. The Training Union develops church members to perform as members of the body of Christ. Not only the purposes make a difference between the Sunday school and Training Union but also the areas of content in their study programs. A school of medicine has a certain body of content and a certain constituency. A school of law has a different body of content and, therefore, a different constituency. In order to understand the Training Union better, let us consider the areas of content which constitute its study programs.

I. INTERPRET SYSTEMATIC THEOLOGY, CHRISTIAN ETHICS, CHRISTIAN HISTORY, AND CHURCH POLITY AND ORGANIZATION

Baptist church members know more than they are given credit for knowing. But they have not spent sufficient time in systematizing what they know. The great concepts of our faith must be learned and understood fully by all Baptist church members. It is generally agreed that only a small percentage of Baptist church members have a clear-cut understanding of why they are Baptists and how they should serve as church members.

1. *Interpret Systematic Theology*

The word "theology" comes from the Greek *theos* meaning God and *logos* meaning study. Theology means the science or discipline which concerns God and God's relation to his world. Theology is based on the Bible, but the study of the Bible in Sunday school is for the purpose of leading each member to understand, accept, and apply the gospel. In the Training Union, the theological beliefs of Baptists are studied in a systematic way for a sufficient period of time so each church member may understand what he believes and why he believes it.

The major concern of the Training Union is to educate church members to have clear, well-formed concepts of

their theological beliefs. The outlines for these materials should include a systematic study of such subjects as God, Christ, the Holy Spirit, man, sin, salvation, and the church.

2. *Interpret Christian Ethics*

Church members not only should have well-structured theological concepts and convictions, but they also should understand and practice Christian relationships with others. Christian ethics is a systematic approach to the study of a Christian's relationship with others. This study program should cover such areas as the conduct of Christians, principles which govern such conduct, and the use of these principles to gain a greater degree of consistency in Christian conduct. The ethical teachings of Christ constitute the base for planning a systematic study of ethics. A study of Paul's writings contributes to understanding Christian ethics.

The Training Union does not approach its task in the same way the Sunday school does. It does not primarily concern itself with Bible exposition. Rather, it uses biblical passages as bases for understanding proper ethical relationships. Included in such studies are duties to self, one's family, one's state and country, other nations, and other races. Today's difficult social problems are included for study to guide church members in applying the ethics of Christ to solving these problems.

3. *Interpret Christian History*

Christian history has been defined as "the story of the origin, progress and development of the Christian religion, and of its influence upon the world." [1] Christian history constitutes such a large body of content that it is extremely difficult to select the significant content areas which church members need to know. It is impossible for church members to understand what is happening now or to predict what will happen in the future without understanding the course of Christian history.

---

[1] W. J. McGlothlin, *The Course of Christian History* (New York: Macmillan Co., 1918), p. 1.

Christian history has been studied little, if any, by the average church member. The time has come for a concerted effort to gain a more comprehensive knowledge of the progress of Christianity from the resurrection of Christ to the present. Laymen, as well as pastors, should be acquainted with Christian history.

Baptist church members need to concentrate upon Baptist history, but they lack true perspective if they do not understand their history in keeping with the general course of Christian history. The vast array of content to be covered should in no way frighten Baptists from the task of becoming better informed in this subject. What is needed is an interpretive presentation of the important events in Christian history in order to help church members understand their rootage in the past and to interpret the present and the future.

Areas to be studied include the beginnings of historical Christianity, the opposition to Christianity by the pagans, the development of the papal system, the Reformation, the period of rationalism, and the period of secularization. A study of Christian history should include a comprehensive study of missions. The Training Union should provide studies in this content area which will improve the missionary understanding of Baptists. Such studies must be planned at the Convention level to relate properly to the study areas of Woman's Missionary Union and the Brotherhood.

4. *Interpret Church Polity and Organization*

Another important study program of the Training Union is church polity and organization. Church polity is the principles of government by which church organization is established and directed. Church organization is the way people are related in a systematic and purposeful arrangement to work toward accomplishing objectives. This study should include also the way the churches organize themselves and function through associations, state conventions, and the Southern Baptist Convention.

A study of church polity and organization is greatly

needed if Baptists are to understand the principles upon which their church organization is based and the ways in which church and denominational organizations function.

The scope of this study program includes the polity and organization of other denominations also. Baptists need to understand their religious neighbors better. They need to know how they organize their churches and conduct their work. It is only through these understandings that Baptists can be committed intelligently to their own beliefs and practices and at the same time work effectively with their fellow Christians.

This study program covers such broad areas as the authority of Jesus Christ, man's relationship to Christ, the priesthood of the believer, and the nature and functions of a church.

A study of church organization should cover such categories as the congregational form of church government; the responsibilities of pastors, staff members, deacons, and other church officers and committees; and principles of church and educational administration.

II. Give Orientation to New Church Members

After a number of years of unprecedented success in winning persons to Christ, Southern Baptists are now being asked, Where are the converts? Southern Baptists have led the world in evangelism, but they have not kept all of those who have been won. Even though our Sunday school enrolment is the highest in the world, it is estimated that only one out of four Southern Baptists attends Sunday school on a given Sunday. No other denomination has the equivalent of the Training Union. Yet even with this organization there is a continuing shortage of workers. It is estimated that only one out of seven Southern Baptists is in Training Union on a given Sunday night.

Southern Baptists' concept of Christian discipleship, the church, and church membership is still a limited one when compared with the concepts of the New Testament. These factors have caused the churches to request assistance in

introducing their new members to the opportunities and responsibilities of church membership. The response to this request is the new church member orientation program.

1. *Objectives*

In new church member orientation, a church is concerned with both new Christians and transfer members. Though needs may vary with different individuals, the basic objective of orientation is the same for all new members in both groups. It is to lead each new member to make his commitment to Christ and the church and to strive diligently for Christian maturity as called for in the New Testament. More specifically it is:

(1) To help each new member understand and reaffirm his conversion experience and his commitment to Christ and the church

(2) To help each new member understand and accept the privileges and responsibilities of membership in the church

(3) To help each new member begin to appropriate the resources of the Christian life and become a growing part of the Christian fellowship through involvement in the life of the church during and beyond the orientation period

2. *Scope*

The scope of new church member orientation may be defined in terms of the persons involved, the content of the program, the activities, and the external relations.

The persons included are (1) all new church members, both new Christians and transfers of all ages; (2) the leaders whom the church elects to serve its new members—namely, the pastor, orientation teachers, selected deacons, and the organizational leaders for the new member's age group; and (3) the members who make up the church which the new member joins.

The content includes the following subjects: (1) the source and nature of the new life in Christ, (2) the nature and mission of the church, and (3) the opportunities for

growth and service which the church provides and encourages.

Activities which make up the orientation program are (1) instruction, (2) counseling, (3) guided reading, (4) guided participation, (5) family involvement, and (6) special program emphases such as fellowship dinners, retreats, and other activities designed to promote the personal involvement of each new member in the life of the church.

A fourth scope-defining factor is external relations. New church member orientation is a task which a church assigns to its Training Union. The Training Union accomplishes this task in co-operation with the home and the other organizations within the church. Finally, the church and the denomination look to new church member orientation for the new member's basic preparation for participation in the church fellowship and its program for growth and service.

III. TRAIN CHURCH MEMBERS TO PERFORM THE FUNCTIONS OF THEIR CHURCH

To train church members means to develop them to become skilful, proficient, and self-disciplined in performing the functions of their church. Church members become trained by proper instruction and by practicing their tasks in order to perform them skilfully. This training is a major responsibility of the Training Union. Through this task, the Training Union assists the church in carrying out the Great Commission of Christ: "Teaching them to observe all things whatsoever I have commanded you" (Matt. 28:20). When a church fails to follow through with a continuous program of instruction for its members, it is failing in its total task of evangelism. Christian conversion can be instantaneous, but Christian growth is a process. Spiritual birth must be followed by spiritual growth. Each church should be both an obstetrician and a pediatrician. The growth of Christian concepts and ideas following the conversion experience often is slow and continues over a lifetime. Thus, every church

must be a school in practical Christian living, and every church member should enrol in this school for his lifetime.

There are basic responsibilities which must be the concern of every church member if a church is to survive, to say nothing of becoming strong. If a church constantly wins people to Christ but does not take time to train them to become responsible church members, it can in time become a disorganized mob. What, then, are some of the major responsibilities of church members?

Every church member should accept his own responsibility for attending the services of his church; praying and reading the Bible daily; actively engaging in private and corporate worship; giving his time, money, and influence; witnessing; studying; ministering; being useful as a citizen; and taking his rightful place in his family. Each church member should be trained to accept these responsibilities regardless of whether he is visited by the pastor, noticed by his fellow church members, or receives public recognition for faithful service.

If a person joins a church for social status, to please some member of his family, or for any other reason than to express his acceptance of Christ as Saviour and Lord, he is a member of a church under false pretenses.

The Training Union seeks not only to provide the finest study materials covering these areas of responsibility but also to lead church members to study and to participate in other purposeful activities. As the Sunday school leads each church member to assist in reaching prospects, to witness daily, and to minister to the needs of individuals, the Training Union is at work training church members to perform these responsibilities. Thus, the program of a church is synchronized and co-ordinated so that all its power is mobilized and channeled in the same direction. The church as a functioning body uses the Sunday school and Training Union to accomplish most of its major tasks. In the church's task of missions, Woman's Missionary Union and the Brotherhood have major responsibilities.

IV. Discover, Recruit, and Give General Training to Potential Leaders of the Church

A church's training program should produce leaders for the church. In a democratic form of church government, both trained leaders and trained followers are necessary. Church members are not trained adequately unless they are trained in the ability to select leaders who will guide them to achieve goals which they find desirable.

1. *Discover Potential Leaders*

The pressing need of every church is trained leaders. A few churches have conquered this problem and have a waiting list of adequately trained leaders. Most churches, however, deal with leadership on a crisis basis—never ready to replace leaders or fill new positions.

Unless some organization is charged with the responsibility of recruiting and giving general training to potential leaders, a church will not have the number or quality of leaders it needs. In practically every church there are enough potential leaders to do the work which the church needs to have done. It is only natural that every person thinks his church is the exception to the rule.

It takes spiritual insight and imagination to discover potential leaders. Jesus found a potential leader in a tree. His first words to him were "Zacchaeus, make haste, and come down" (Luke 19:5). Jesus' command continued in a request for a conference in Zacchaeus' home.

When Jesus saw Simon Peter, he thought, not in terms of what Simon Peter was, but in terms of what he was to become. Jesus said to him, "Thou art Simon the son of Jona: thou shalt be called Cephas, which is by interpretation, A stone" (John 1:42).

As potential leaders in the church begin to emerge, they should be recruited and given additional opportunities for development.

2. *Recruit Potential Leaders*

The Training Union is responsible for recruiting potential

leaders for training. A church should use a nominating committee to recommend leaders for election. But this committee will need a reservoir of potential leaders from which to select those who will be recommended. An annual election does not solve leadership problems. A volunteer organization is constantly changing in leadership. While attempts should be made to stabilize its leadership, a church must also give considerable thought to planning for an adequate supply of workers.

The Training Union should survey not only its own Adult and Young People's unions for potential leaders but also the other organizations of the church. Teachers of Adult and Young People's classes in the Sunday school, the president and youth directors of Woman's Missionary Union, the president and other officers of the Brotherhood, the deacons, and other church leaders should be surveyed periodically for recommendations of potential leaders.

Care should be taken in offering positions of leadership to younger Young People. Age and maturity, however, are not synonymous. Young People who have grown up in Christian homes and have been educated by their churches often are more adequately equipped to serve than older Adults. Altruistic impulses often prompt Intermediates and younger Young People to offer themselves for service. As a rule, Intermediates should not be used. In most cases, seventeen- and eighteen-year-old Young People should be encouraged to stay in their classes and unions for further preparation there. Young People of other ages may be used effectively when they have been adequately prepared and when they have been counseled as to the obligations and responsibilities which they must assume as workers in their churches.

3. *Train Potential Leaders*

The Training Union is responsible for giving general training to potential leaders. General training includes instruction and practice in basic principles and methods of education and administration. These are two broad areas

of content which further expand the study programs of the Training Union. Instruction in these areas will take place in various ways. Some training will occur on Sunday evening. But much general training must be given at other times. Special conferences and clinics with practical laboratory experience may be used during the week to train potential leaders. In these areas the Training Union is not basically concerned with giving instruction in its own principles and methods. Rather, it exists for the church and utilizes these opportunities to give broad basic training to equip potential leaders for places of service in a church.

Preparing parents to teach and train their children is one of the most important of all church tasks. Parents are the greatest group of potential leaders a church has. The church that succeeds in training parents to guide the religious growth of their children has captured its greatest potential for Christian education. Christian homes can become dynamic schools of Christian education if parents understand their roles and prepare adequately for them.

The Training Union trains parents to be Christian teachers in their homes. This training strengthens the entire base of Christian education in the church and establishes the home on a solid foundation.

Let us now contrast general training with specific training so as to sharpen the differences in these areas of responsibility. The Sunday school, Brotherhood, Woman's Missionary Union, and Music Ministry give specific training to their workers. The content of this specific training is set forth in categories 17, 19, and 20 in the Church Study Course. The Training Union offers its services to each of these organizations as needed in arranging for time, a teacher, and textbooks for special training efforts.

The Training Union gives special promotion to the study of Training Union books listed in category 18 of the Church Study Course. It assists the other church organizations as needed in the promotion of the study of their books as listed in categories 17, 19, and 20. It also assists in the training of church officers and committee members using books in

category 16. Of course, all church organizations participating in the Church Study Course promote the study of all books in the course, but the Training Union should give special attention to the study of books in the general categories.

The Training Union has the responsibility for keeping study course records for the church or for seeing that this is done. In many instances, these records can be kept by the general secretary of the Training Union or by someone else appointed specifically for this purpose. Churches with church secretaries or educational secretaries may place this responsibility upon such a worker.

V. PROVIDE ORGANIZATION AND LEADERSHIP FOR SPECIAL PROJECTS OF THE CHURCH

Providing organization and leadership for special projects of the church is a task of the Training Union and except for the projects involved is similar to this task of the Sunday school. These responsibilities which involve the two major educational programs of a church do not mean a duplication of activities. The nature of the Sunday school has caused churches to delegate to it certain responsibilities. The nature of the Training Union has caused the churches to delegate to it certain other responsibilities. Both the Sunday school and the Training Union are to provide organization and leadership for special projects of the church.

The Training Union makes its greatest contribution to the churches through its ongoing educational program. But there are special short-term projects which the Training Union is especially fitted to conduct for a church.

Most churches now have a period of training conducted by the Training Union prior to special revival meetings. The Training Union offers the study of textbooks and resource units showing church members how to witness for Christ. Many churches supplement the textbook study with practical experience in visiting unsaved prospects.

Quite often a church requests its Training Union to conduct a study course on stewardship prior to the subscription

of the church budget. Through this study each member will be instructed in how to relate the giving of his money to the broader base of the stewardship of life.

The associational Training Union organization annually conducts a one-night training clinic for church officers and committee members. Larger churches with trained leaders conduct their own clinics by assigning this responsibility to their Training Unions. Those included in this period of special training are clerks, treasurers, trustees, deacons, and members of all church committees. Such training enables a church to begin its year of activities with officers and committee members informed of their responsibilities.

VI. Provide and Interpret Information Regarding the Work of the Church and the Denomination

The pastor, the church staff, and the Training Union director should consult with the Training Union leaders regarding information which should be interpreted. The method and time should likewise be considered. The time of the general and department assembly periods should not be taken in simply making announcements regarding various activities of the church. The significant tasks of the church should be singled out, and time should be given to interpreting them appropriately. In this way the Training Union not only serves as a church educational organization but also becomes a channel for interpreting to its members the life and work of the church.

The Training Union Department of the Sunday School Board, like the Sunday School Department, is one of the channel departments. It not only discovers, develops, and interprets the program of Training Union work for Southern Baptists but also interprets through its regular materials and programs the work of other Southern Baptist Convention boards, agencies, and institutions.

The Training Union enrolment of Southern Baptist churches is second only to the Sunday school. The Training Union organization functions in three fourths of Southern Baptist churches. Whatever Southern Baptists want to say

regularly to the second largest number of people can be said best through the Training Union.

In order to carry a balanced program of education to all church members, the Training Union Department co-operates with other departments of the Sunday School Board and with other Southern Baptist boards, agencies, and institutions so as to relate each of them properly to the planning of Training Union materials and program suggestions.

For this reason the Training Union Department carries in its magazine and lesson course materials information regarding other Southern Baptist Convention agencies. It also interprets the work of associations and state conventions. The Training Union Department thus becomes the Convention's best agency for interpreting to the churches the objectives and program responsibilities of its agencies.

As the Training Union Department's long-range plan for developing materials and programs suggestions is implemented, it can provide a balanced course of study and an interpretation of programs and materials not possible by any other organization.

CHAPTER 6

I. TEACH MISSIONS AND PRAY FOR MISSIONS
   1. Teach the Missionary Message of the Bible
   2. Teach the Course of Christian Missions
   3. Teach Contemporary Missions
   4. Pray for Missions

II. PROVIDE ORGANIZATION AND LEADERSHIP FOR SPECIAL MISSIONS PROJECTS OF THE CHURCH
   1. Give to Missions
   2. Render Missionary Service in the Community

III. PROVIDE AND INTERPRET INFORMATION REGARDING THE WORK OF THE CHURCH AND THE DENOMINATION

Lead people to participate

6

The Task of
WOMAN'S MISSIONARY UNION

WOMAN'S MISSIONARY UNION is the church's educational organization for providing missionary education for children, girls, young women, and adult women. The organizations are Sunbeam Band for young children, Girls' Auxiliary for Junior and Intermediate girls, Young Woman's Auxiliary for young women, and Woman's Missionary Society for adult women.

Woman's Missionary Union is third in total membership among the church educational organizations. It also ranks third among these organizations in the number of churches in which it functions.

From its beginning until the present, Woman's Missionary Union has not changed its major objectives and program responsibilities: to promote Christian missions through mission study, prayer, community missions, and stewardship.

I. TEACH MISSIONS AND PRAY FOR MISSIONS

Since Woman's Missionary Union specializes in missionary education, its study program consists of the missionary message of the Bible and the course of Christian missions, including contemporary missions.

1. *Teach the Missionary Message of the Bible*

Missions cannot be understood adequately without under-

standing the missionary message of the Bible. Therefore, the study program of Woman's Missionary Union includes content which reveals God's missionary purpose for all persons. The missionary message of the Bible begins with the Old Testament. Woman's Missionary Union plans for the study of God's missionary plan from the Old Testament through the entire Bible.

The Old Testament reveals missions in the plan of God. Man's sin is the reason for missions. Abraham has been referred to as the first missionary. He was chosen as an agent in God's missionary plan. Abraham became a foreign missionary, for he left his own people to live in a country of God's own choice.

The prophets were messengers of world missions. Since their messages are rich in missionary content, the prophets should receive attention in planning for the study of missions in the Bible. These messages reveal the universality and the love of God and his desire to bring all nations into a knowledge of his love and purpose.

The New Testament offers the richest field of study for missionary education. The coming of Christ, the establishment of his church, and the launching of the Christian missionary enterprise make the New Testament a story of world missions. In their Gospels, Matthew and Luke relate the birth of Christ, but these are records of his incarnation. The Gospel of John indicates that Jesus existed with the Father before the creation of the earth.

During the early phases of his ministry, Jesus proclaimed regeneration through repentance and faith available to all men. Later he established his church with a universal mission. When his missionary enterprise had been established and just before he returned to the Father, he called his followers to him and commissioned them to give the message of his redemptive purpose to the entire world.

After the coming of the Holy Spirit on the day of Pentecost, the early Christians witnessed with great power and fervor. The New Testament churches were missionary because their members were missionary.

Paul and his missionary journeys constitute another area of study in missionary education. In the first century, Paul became the great exponent of the missionary message of God's love to lost men in all countries. On these journeys he came face to face with the need of sinful men for regeneration.

The Bible is God's missionary message to mankind. Woman's Missionary Union teaches this message to its members.

2. *Teach the Course of Christian Missions*

A study of the missionary message of the Bible gives the basis for the world mission task of Baptists. A study of the course of Christian missions indicates progress which is being made in carrying out the Great Commission of Christ. It is necessary for church members to know the conditions and circumstances under which the gospel has progressed from the ascension of Christ to the present.

Christian history is one of the study programs of the Training Union. The course of Christian missions is a part of the study program of Christian history. Missions though is so important, church organizations are needed to major upon missionary education. Woman's Missionary Union majors on missions. Baptists church members cannot be truly missionary unless they are educated in the need of the world for the gospel of Christ. The close interrelationship of Christian history and Christian missions calls for co-operative curriculum planning at the Southern Baptist Convention level. Proper planning will give to Baptist church members the desirable correlation, balance, comprehensiveness, and sequence for their missionary education materials.

The study of Christian missions should cover the significant events from Pentecost to the present. This can be done both through a general approach and through studying the history of missions in various countries.

Of particular significance to Baptist church members is the history of Baptists missions. Such history should include

an intensive study of missions from the time of William Carey to the present. An important section of this study must be an understanding of the development and progress of foreign missions under the leadership of the Foreign Mission Board of the Southern Baptist Convention.

The origin, development, and progress of Southern Baptists home missions under the direction of the Home Mission Board of the Southern Baptist Convention is of special interest to Baptists. State and associational missions should be studied also if the full missions task and missionary expression of the churches is to be understood.

All such phases of mission study are important and should be known and understood by Baptist church members. However, with such a wealth of materials to study and with limited time to do so, gaining an understanding of this material becomes a major problem. Certain content is studied in regular program materials. Other phases of study find expression in mission study books. In each instance, the approach is that of education through the study of the most important events and emphases in these areas.

3. *Teach Contemporary Missions*

Although study of the biblical and historical material is necessary, a thorough study of the current missionary situation must have full consideration. The situation of missions today and in the future in one's association, state, country, and in countries overseas must be understood. Presenting information and the challenge of mission opportunities in countries where Southern Baptists are not presently working is a task of Woman's Missionary Union also. Southern Baptists need constantly to be informed as to their progress with reference to Christ's command to win a lost world to him. Such materials as mission study books, program publications, general mission books, and mission magazines interpret the contemporary world scene and its challenge. Woman's Missionary Union has the task of keeping its members informed of the urgency in carrying out the Great Commission and of the progress made in doing so.

A study of missions would be incomplete without a study of missionary biography. A study of missionary personalities often gives more understanding of missions than a study of dates and events. Missionaries are not persons to be held in awe and wonder; they are persons to know, love, and appreciate. The dedication of missionary personnel, their accomplishments under difficulty and their willingness to sacrifice—all constitute thrilling chapters of missionary education.

Appeals for money often are made before people understand their relationship to the world missions task of Christ. Most churches have not given their members the basic understandings of the stewardship of life out of which proper offerings come. Many Southern Baptist church members are still confined in thought and action to their own neighborhoods. They are more concerned with themselves and their neighbors than with the needs of the multitudes of lost persons around the world. Woman's Missionary Union serves to cause church members to lift up their eyes and look upon the fields.

Southern Baptists have been criticized for giving so little money to missions. They have been compared unfavorably with other denominations and have been accused of being narrow and self-centered in their outlook. If these criticisms are true, it is because there has not been enough education and information with proper motivation to challenge them to do their best for Christ.

Missionary education is one of the most challenging of all study opportunities in a church. Each church should plan for missionary education to be offered to as many members as possible. Woman's Missionary Union seeks especially to enlist all women and youth, but it supports all church plans for missionary education.

4. Pray for Missions

Study and prayer are inseparable in Woman's Missionary Union. Information is basic to an intelligent prayer life. One cannot pray for definite objects without information

regarding them. The physical, intellectual, social, and spiritual needs of individuals around the world cause any thinking Christian to remember these multitudes of needy persons in prayer. When world needs are great and the money which is received for these needs is meager, one is led to pray that God may use these inadequate gifts as Christ did the loaves and fishes. Certainly without the blessings of God, paltry gifts would never make much impact upon the tremendous needs of the world. One should pray also that new insights into the needs of persons without the gospel will cause Christians to share more of their material resources with them.

Woman's Missionary Union was founded on prayer, has continued its work in the spirit of prayer, and must go forward by prayer in the future.

Prayer is perhaps the most neglected phase of the Christian life. Most church members do not spend sufficient time in prayer. When they do pray, their prayers are so general that they hardly help those who have specific problems needing prayer support. There is value in concerted prayer and in praying for definite objects of need.

Woman's Missionary Union members engage in periods of special prayer during their weeks of prayer for home and foreign missions and their season of prayer for state missions. By remembering definite objects of prayer for foreign, home, and state missions, the prayer potential of thousands of church members is mobilized.

These special weeks of prayer and study are the most significant times for missions each year. One can only wonder what would happen if the entire membership of the church should engage in such special weeks of prayer and study.

Woman's Missionary Union and the Training Union encourage daily prayer for missionaries by name. Missionaries are listed on the prayer calendars according to their birth dates. Their names, work, and fields of service are listed so that prayer for them can be as specific as possible. As we pray for missionaries daily, we can pray that their

insights and experiences may lead them to develop an increasingly effective strategy for meeting the changing needs of their environment.

It is encouraging that an organization in the church has developed its program in a large measure upon periods of study and prayer. Woman's Missionary Union has demonstrated the value of making prayer, as well as study, a significant spiritual experience for each of its members.

II. PROVIDE ORGANIZATION AND LEADERSHIP FOR SPECIAL MISSIONS PROJECTS OF THE CHURCH

In addition to providing missionary education, Woman's Missionary Union serves the churches in other significant ways. One of the most important of these is leading church members to be stewards of their possessions.

1. *Give to Missions*

The giving of money to missions has always been a vital phase of the program of Woman's Missionary Union. To study missions and to pray for missions results in the desire to give to missions. One cannot be missionary unless he shares his material possessions for missionary purposes.

Study and prayer personalize giving. Previously it was pointed out that through study Woman's Missionary Union members are made aware of the needs and problems of mission work. They learn the names and vocations of the missionaries. Thus, instead of their giving being impersonal, Woman's Missionary Union members give to meet definite needs.

There is a vast difference in giving money to the missions item in a church budget and in visualizing such giving as a means of assisting a missionary doctor or nurse in Japan, a theological professor in Taiwan, or a missionary pastor in Argentina.

Knowledge of missionaries—their work and needs—causes Woman's Missionary Union members to give more intelligently to all causes through their church budgets. The

support of the total church budget is vitally supported by Woman's Missionary Union members.

By making the Annie Armstrong, Lottie Moon, and state missions offerings churchwide, Woman's Missionary Union strengthens church and denominational life.

Each church which participates in these offerings finds its interest in, and support of, world missions increasing. Woman's Missionary Union has requested and receives support from the other church educational organizations in the promotion of these churchwide offerings.

Members of this organization also study carefully the Cooperative Program and the causes it includes. Program materials of Woman's Missionary Union carry information regarding the Southern Baptist Convention boards, agencies, and institutions which are supported through the Cooperative Program. Knowledge of their work and needs leads to increased support of the Cooperative Program.

2. *Render Missionary Service in the Community*

Members of Woman's Missionary Union are not satisfied for gifts to missions to represent their total concern for a lost world. Each member of the organization is encouraged to serve Christ and her church by putting forth missionary effort in her own community.

Such effort involves taking part in the church program of witnessing. Members support the ongoing personal witnessing engaged in by the church. They also participate in special revival meetings and other evangelistic activities.

The heart of community missions is personal witnessing. Woman's Missionary Union objectives call for the co-operation of its members in the church program of witnessing. Where churches do not have organized programs, suggestions for witnessing in Woman's Missionary Union materials are followed.

Woman's Missionary Union members likewise serve the church in its program of personal ministries. Through this program, the women of the church serve to alleviate human suffering and to express Christian fellowship. Included in

such ministries are services in jails, hospitals, and other institutions, relief work, and work with persons of other countries who are in the United States. Many of the latter are international students in American colleges and universities.

A further emphasis on community missions deals with strengthening Christian standards in each community. Work among all races, including literacy work, the distribution of Bibles and Christian literature, support of alcohol education, and of activities related to responsible citizenship, are a part of this program.

Woman's Missionary Union members strive to be missionaries in their communities as well as missionaries in the uttermost part of the earth.

III. PROVIDE AND INTERPRET INFORMATION REGARDING THE WORK OF THE CHURCH AND THE DENOMINATION

Woman's Missionary Union serves the churches as an agent of communication. Communication is a major problem in every organization. A Baptist church is no exception. It takes a long time to inform church members of various projects and emphases as well as programs to which they should be vitally related. Officers in Woman's Missionary Union, by keeping in close contact with the pastor and other workers of the church, give great assistance in informing the members of their organization as to church plans and programs. This organization through its leaders magnifies the total program of the church and gives first consideration to its life and work. By interpreting information for its church, each Woman's Missionary Union organization fulfils its task in an effective way.

The president of Woman's Missionary Union as a member of the church council is in a position to know the total church program and to assist in interpreting it to the leaders and members of WMU. She should reserve time in the general meetings of the organization to interpret the broad aspects of the church's program to the members. They must be led to see the church as the body of Christ, with many

members, each one of which must function properly if Christ's work is to be done in a significant way. Such special occasions as revivals, church budget subscriptions, church building campaigns, Sunday school enlargement campaigns, and special weeks of study should be presented and given full support. Any matter which concerns the church must be the concern of each church organization.

Circle chairmen should be given information regarding church activities so that it may be shared with Woman's Missionary Union members in their circle meetings. Keeping members informed of their church's work can involve them in the basic actions which the church will take throughout the year.

Although it majors on missionary education, Woman's Missionary Union is valuable both to the churches and to the denomination in interpreting information regarding other programs. Through its periodicals, it interprets the programs of other Southern Baptist Convention boards, agencies, and institutions. Such information is, in addition to the regular program materials, studied by members of this organization. It assists Southern Baptist Convention agencies which do not have organization in the states and associations to carry their programs to the churches.

A case in point is the Stewardship Commission of the Southern Baptist Convention. This commission was established to co-ordinate and promote activities related to church finance and the Cooperative Program. Although states have promotional secretaries for stewardship, these secretaries do not have a special associational or church organization through which to work. Woman's Missionary Union can both interpret the work of this commission and assist other church organizations, such as the Sunday school and Training Union, in providing an educational base for the Stewardship Commission's promotional activities.

Every Baptist church will find that its task of growing a missionary church will be accomplished much more readily and effectively if it supports and utilizes its Woman's Missionary Union.

Of major importance is the role of Woman's Missionary Union in communicating the programs of the Home Mission Board and the Foreign Mission Board. In addition to program materials which interpret the actual mission work engaged in by these boards, Woman's Missionary Union materials interpret the manner in which these boards are organized and function. Woman's Missionary Union members are informed of the plan of operation of these agencies, their financial requirements for program operations, and the unmet needs which they face.

Such information not only personalizes those who serve in these agencies but also causes Woman's Missionary Union members to become identified personally with the missionaries who serve under the appointment of these boards.

CHAPTER 7

I. TEACH MISSIONS TO BOYS, YOUNG MEN, AND MEN
   1. Teach Missions to Boys
   2. Teach Missions to Young Men
   3. Teach Missions to Men

II. PROVIDE ORGANIZATION AND LEADERSHIP FOR SPECIAL MISSIONS PROJECTS OF THE CHURCH
   1. Provide Missions Projects for Young Men
   2. Provide Missions Projects for Men

III. PROVIDE AND INTERPRET INFORMATION REGARDING THE WORK OF THE CHURCH AND THE DENOMINATION

Lead people to participate.

7

The Task of
THE BROTHERHOOD

WHEN the Brotherhood began in 1907 as the Layman's Missionary Movement, its purpose was to stimulate the zeal and activity of laymen to a more thorough consecration of their time, prayer, and means to the glory of God in worldwide evangelism. A prime object of the movement was the enlistment of men in the affairs of Christ's kingdom. It was a systematic effort on the part of those laymen who had a constraining vision to bring the great mass of laymen face to face with their religious obligation. It was an appeal to laymen from the standpoint of laymen. It urged men to pray daily, study diligently, plan wisely, serve zealously, and give generously that the kingdom of Christ might prosper.

Later it was thought wise to change the name of the organization both to give it a wider scope of work and to make clear that the organization included pastors as well as laymen.

However, the heart of the Brotherhood work has always been missions and missionary education. Thus, in recent years it has turned more to its original objectives, so that now it carries the responsibility for missionary education for boys, young men, and men. Such education seeks to develop a Christlike concern for all peoples, an intimate knowledge of how Christian fellowship is being extended at

home and abroad, and a hearty participation in all efforts
to enlarge this fellowship of Christian faith until it covers
the earth. Like other church educational organizations, it
has a distinctive study program and activities.

I. TEACH MISSIONS TO BOYS, YOUNG MEN, AND MEN

The Brotherhood has a study program similar to Woman's
Missionary Union. But the content of the program is chosen
to interest and challenge the male members of the church
in becoming missionary Baptists. Since the Brotherhood
majors on missions and missionary education, it is advan-
tageous to examine the meanings of these terms.

The word "missions" comes from the Latin verb *missio,*
which means to send. It refers both to those sent and to
those who send. It is missionary not only to be sent but also
to send.

Missions is central in the Bible. The Bible interprets God
as a God of love and mercy. He provides for man in his
fallen condition and urges those who have been redeemed
to proclaim the good news of salvation to all men everywhere.

God's desire is for this message to be known by every
human being in the world (see John 17 : 23). For this reason every Christian is a missionary sent by God to the rest
of the human race to proclaim the gospel (see Luke 24 :
47–48).

Missions, then, is what church members do to extend the
gospel beyond the congregation. It is a church reaching out
into its immediate community and into the world beyond
to share with all men what God has done for them through
Jesus Christ. Missions is the ceaseless demonstration of
God's redeeming love expressed through Christian service
to the total personalities of men everywhere. In such a concept, care must be taken not to become spiritually short-
sighted and concentrate exclusively upon one's own immediate community. A church must think in world terms if it
is to be truly missionary. It must lead its members to work
as far as they can go geographically and then lead them to

let their financial resources take over for them at that point. Their gifts support their representatives who are specifically called to work in distant lands or in nearby associations or states where it is impossible for them to serve. Churches also should be concerned that God should call out from their members volunteers for appointment as missionaries to other lands. A church is a missionary force, and the world is its field.

Missionary education is that part of Christian education which majors upon interpreting the missionary message of the Bible and the course of Christian missions. Involved in this education is an understanding of world needs and a readiness to meet these needs. Basic also is an enlarging knowledge of other races and groups and a willingness to share with them the highest Christian values we possess. Missionary education seeks also to develop attitudes toward other peoples on the other side of town or the other side of the world in keeping with the love of Christ for all men. Information covering such areas causes persons to become familiar with needs and to organize to meet these needs.

Missionary education must first produce results in the lives of church members. After that, church members will seek to produce results in the lives of others in various parts of the world.

Missionary education begins with the right knowledge of God and of Christ's love and purpose for all men. Its aim is that of producing Christians who will have a conscious fellowship with Christ and a desire to share his purpose with the world.

The content of the study program of the Brotherhood is God's missionary purpose for mankind as expressed in the Bible and a knowledge of how the Christian message has been shared with the world since Christ's return to the Father. The study of the progress of the spread of the gospel is made in such a way that boys, young men, and men are challenged to share in the extension of Christ's kingdom on earth. A continuing emphasis is placed upon the need to develop and channel the concern of Baptist men to an ap-

plication of their faith through service in their church, community, and world.

1. Teach Missions to Boys

The Brotherhood has the assignment of missionary education of boys nine years of age and above, and conducts a study program for them in keeping with their needs. This program provides experiences for boys in group participation, individual advancement, relationships with other people, and service projects.

Boys as a rule are friendly with each other regardless of class, race, or creed. Prejudice is usually passed from parent to child. If boys are given the proper education and guidance, their good will toward others will become a strong base upon which the love of one's fellow man may be based in mature adulthood.

They also have a normal and natural interest in people of other lands. They are interested in their appearance, their mode of dress, their food, their habits of living, and their language.

Many boys are responsive to the needs of persons close at home. Their study of the Bible and of the needs of persons who need the ministry and service of their churches constitute powerful areas of learning for this age group.

These characteristics of boys make it both necessary and desirable to provide adequate missionary education for them.

2. Teach Missions to Young Men

A church's missionary education program for young men should be developed upon its missionary education program for boys. Of equal appeal to young men are the missionary message of the Bible, the needs of persons at home and abroad, and the expression of Christian good will to all nations.

It is particularly important for young men to understand the needs which exist for missionary personnel. The Brotherhood has a unique opportunity and ministry in making

clear to the young men of Southern Baptist churches the need of associations, states, home missions, and overseas missions for volunteers. Although many volunteers have made their decisions for mission work during childhood, most make their decisions during adolescence. The Brotherhood renders invaluable service to young men by giving information regarding the growing needs of the denomination for skilled, trained leaders in many areas of service.

While some young men will volunteer, prepare, and be appointed to serve as missionaries, the vast majority of them will serve their churches in the homeland and make it possible for those who volunteer to go. For this reason it is important that missionary education of young men include a clear interpretation of the needs on mission fields which must be met through financial support. They need to know what is involved in the support of missionaries. They need to be informed as to the capital needs of missionary activity. It is important also for them to know what could be done if more funds were made available for the extension of mission work. The Brotherhood majors upon making clear the needs of overseas missions, since it is somewhat easier to understand missions needs close at hand.

Of importance also is the proper interpretation of what young men can do through their churches in their own communities. A church which becomes a strong missionary force locally is more likely to produce mission volunteers and dynamic Christian leaders than a church which takes its missionary opportunities for granted.

3. Teach Missions to Men

Men need to know the biblical basis for missions and the history of Christian missions from the time of Christ to the present. They need to understand the areas where missionary action takes place, such as in their associations and states; and they need to know the areas served by the Home Mission Board and the Foreign Mission Board.

Men need instruction in missions today. They are greatly interested in current events. They read newspapers and news

magazines. By using imagination, insight, and sufficient skills, those responsible for missionary education in the churches will find that pictures, maps, and illustrations from newspapers and magazines are useful in extending the missionary knowledge of men.

The Brotherhood through its discussion groups and seminars is rendering invaluable service in bringing men together in small groups to learn about the needs of the world and to discuss their part in meeting these needs.

Of particular value to men is a study of missions in the future. It is possible that men do not realize that mission work in every area of the world needs to be expanded immediately. The budgets of associations, states, the Home Mission Board, and the Foreign Mission Board represent only the basic minimum needs. The work of Christ around the world could be expanded greatly if men understood the needs that exist and willingly invested their money in the expansion of the kingdom of Christ.

It is important for men as fathers to know the needs of Southern Baptists for missionary personnel. As their sons and daughters volunteer for missions, parents can give encouragement and guidance to them in preparing for their tasks.

By being aware of the needs of their immediate communities, men will be better able to take the initiative in establishing missions and in rendering other missionary service to their communities.

II. Provide Organization and Leadership for Special Missions Projects of the Church

The learnings experienced in the Brotherhood through study should be further expanded through related learning activities.

1. *Provide Missions Projects for Young Men*

Many missions projects of the church need the assistance of young men. Young men can be used to conduct mission

Vacation Bible schools. Some projects are particularly appealing to college students. Needy communities may be located, and the Brotherhood can challenge young men to participate in conducting mission Vacation Bible schools in these areas.

Young men also may be led to volunteer for student summer missions. The Baptist Student Union and the Home Mission Board have worked together in fostering summer mission work for many years. The Brotherhood can challenge young men to participate in this work and to report to their churches when they return from their activities at the close of each summer. If a church will capitalize upon the contacts made by its young men during the summer months, a spirit of missions can be created within the congregation. If young men are sent out as representatives of their churches during this period, the church can broaden its base of missionary operation. Likewise, the young men involved will feel that they are rendering missionary service for their churches.

The Brotherhood also can lead young men to make the most of missionary opportunities through military service. When young men are called to serve their country, they should be encouraged to give a positive Christian witness wherever they go. If this opportunity is rightly presented to young men, it can become a missionary project for the church.

Likewise, young men who go overseas as representatives of business concerns in this country may prove to be truly missionary. If they are given special recognition by their churches and encouraged to look for opportunities to be of service for Christ, the church can greatly enlarge the scope of its ministry. Many young men who leave their home churches and go into other parts of the United States find almost as many opportunities for mission work as if they had gone overseas. The Brotherhood by calling attention to all of these opportunities serves to challenge young men to be missionary wherever they are.

2. Provide Missions Projects for Men

For many years Brotherhoods have been useful to their churches in starting new churches and missions. Members of the Brotherhood have worked on church missions committees and have served to locate places where new missions and churches are needed. Many Brotherhood members have donated materials and labor to build new church buildings, chapels, and meeting places for missions. There are men in most churches who will not teach or take other positions of leadership. They will, however, do what their interests and talents lead them to do. This means that a church's local mission program offers many opportunities to employ the resources of men who otherwise would not be enlisted in some other phase of church work.

The Brotherhood in most Southern Baptist churches observes in January *Baptist Men's Day*. This project enables the Brotherhood to call attention to the part that men can play in the church's work.

The Brotherhood can serve the church by leading men to visit places during their vacation trips each year where state and home missions work is being conducted. If such visits are planned carefully, the church may hear reports of places visited when families return from their vacations. These firsthand learning contacts are among the most valuable a church may have. Carried out from year to year, they will build great missionary interest and information.

A Brotherhood can assist the church in carrying out missions projects by encouraging the church to set apart businessmen to represent Christ as they travel to other lands. Many Baptist businessmen are making foreign trips each year. Most churches are overlooking a real missionary opportunity in not setting apart these men to be special representatives of their churches as they travel in other lands. Such men could be informed about the location of mission work and could visit with missionary personnel in the various countries. In conversation with missionaries they could become better acquainted with the needs on the

mission fields and could report the needs to their churches upon their return.

The Brotherhood Commission has rendered Southern Baptist churches a unique service by enlisting Brotherhood members for mission tours to other lands. These Brotherhood members have paid their own expenses. As they have traveled, they have made wonderful impressions for good upon the nationals in the countries they have visited. They also have given encouragement to missionaries and national leaders through their contacts.

The Brotherhood Commission has organized teams of men to go into pioneer areas in the United States to assist the churches there in establishing missions and in strengthening their work. By sharing in this type of home mission work these men have become enthusiastic regarding home missions and have been deeply motivated. This type of activity is gaining enthusiastic support and in time should prove to be one of the greatest missionary factors in the growth of Southern Baptist work.

The Brotherhood can assist the churches by encouraging men to make the most of their mission opportunities as they serve in the armed forces. Many men are making the armed services a career. The valuable opportunities and contacts of these men can count for Christ as they use their opportunities for maximum Christian witness.

In addition, Brotherhoods in churches near service installations may work with the chaplains and military personnel in special projects where their assistance is needed and requested.

III. PROVIDE AND INTERPRET INFORMATION REGARDING THE WORK OF THE CHURCH AND THE DENOMINATION

The Brotherhood not only serves to educate boys, young men, and men in missions; it also interprets to them basic information regarding the work of their church and denomination. It is extremely important for the Brotherhood to interpret the total church program to men and boys. Most men are busy to the point of being absorbed in their vo-

cations. So many things clamor for their attention that they become immune to church appeals. The Brotherhood fills a vital need by presenting the work of the church to the men and boys in such a way that they will understand and readily respond to it.

A special need in interpreting the work of the church and the denomination to boys is to present the information in such a way that they will feel involved in the work. If boys can be led to recognize and understand the ways in which their churches need them, they will respond readily. They will respond also when denominational information is presented in the right way.

Men have been slow to take their rightful places in the life of their churches. In most cases the major difficulty grows out of the fact that they are uninformed. Information presented properly and with right motivation can be an influencing factor in bringing them to a more loyal support of their churches.

Men communicating with men can convey this information effectively. One of the prime values in having an organization for men is that there can be this effective communication of information.

Through its materials, the Brotherhood also interprets information regarding the work of the denomination. It, too, is a channel organization and is useful in interpreting information regarding the denominational program to its constituency. Constant attention to helping men become acquainted with the work of their church and denomination is given both through Brotherhood literature and suggested activities.

The Brotherhood Commission of the Southern Baptist Convention is alert to the phases of denominational life and emphases of the Convention which are important for men to understand and support.

The personnel of the Commission are in touch with the personnel of other Convention agencies responsible for planning curriculum and program suggestions. Therefore, the Brotherhood Commission can include in its materials

the significant information needed by Southern Baptist men. The Brotherhood provides a choice opportunity for the church to provide special approaches for the participation of men in evangelism, stewardship, and missions.

Such information assists the churches in keeping their men abreast of Convention programing, problems, needs, and progress. Informed laymen are the hope of the churches. In the area of communications, the Brotherhood makes one of its most significant contributions.

CHAPTER 8

I. TEACH MUSIC
1. To Choir Members
2. To Song Leaders and Instrumentalists
3. To the Congregation

II. TRAIN PERSONS TO LEAD, SING, AND PLAY MUSIC

III. LEAD PERSONS TO PARTICIPATE IN HYMN SINGING AND TO UNDERSTAND HYMNODY

IV. ASSIST THE CHURCH IN ITS FUNCTIONS
1. To Worship
2. To Proclaim
3. To Educate
4. To Minister

V. PROVIDE AND INTERPRET INFORMATION REGARDING THE WORK OF THE CHURCH AND THE DENOMINATION

8

The Task of
THE MUSIC MINISTRY

THE MUSIC MINISTRY is the organization which the church establishes to teach music; to train its members to lead, sing, and play music; to participate in hymn singing; to understand hymnody; and to assist in the functions of worship, proclamation, education, and ministry. The Music Ministry includes congregational, choral, and instrumental training and other activities extending to all areas of church life. It is designed to include learning experiences for all church members and their children. It is established by vote of the church, and those who serve in places of leadership are elected to their positions by the church.

The membership of the Music Ministry includes all persons engaged in the music program of a church, such as the pastor, the minister of music or director of music, the church organist and pianist, other staff members, song leaders, pianists, members of all choirs and ensembles, members of instrumental ensembles and orchestras, choir sponsors, and music council members. A church has a Music Ministry when it elects a person to lead its music, uses music to strengthen its functions, and has one or more music groups which meet regularly.

It has been difficult for some to understand why the music program should be organized in churches, associations, state conventions, and the Southern Baptist Convention. This

organizational approach to the program of church music was established by the Southern Baptist Convention in 1944. The decision reached in the 1944 Convention grew out of seven intensive years of study by a special committee. The Convention accepted the committee's report and projected a Convention-wide church music program on an organized basis. The following excerpts are from the recommendations of the committee on church music and worship:

> We can't have better Church Music until we train our people. . . .
> We note with satisfaction the growing tendency on the part of States, Associations, and Churches to do something definite about Church Music. . . .
> We reaffirm our belief in the graded choirs. . . .
> We urge our Baptist Colleges, Universities, and Seminaries to place in their curriculum a Department of Church Music and that certain, definite courses be required of all ministerial students. . . .
> We urge States to consider a Church Music set-up equal in scope, etc., to the other departments of Church activity fostered by our states. . . .
> We feel that Southern Baptists are justified in asking that a considerable amount of the profits received from the sale of song books and other music be expended in a worthy Church Music Educational Program. Therefore, realizing the dire need of, and the Macedonian call for, a better Church Music Program for Southern Baptists, we recommend that the Sunday School Board be instructed to increase the personnel of the Department of Church Music sufficiently to prepare and set going a constructive, educational program of Church Music among Southern Baptists.[1]

The Convention action can be attributed to a number of factors. Through the years, Southern Baptist churches have been the victims of various individuals and groups who have used music as a means of getting into the churches, commercializing sacred music, and often leading some of the churches out of the denomination.

---

[1] *Annual of the Southern Baptist Convention: 1944* (Executive Committee, Southern Baptist Convention), pp. 146-47.

Also, people are influenced by the music they sing. No denomination can rise above its hymnody. The quality of the music and the words of songs and hymns greatly influence the theological beliefs and general church life of those who sing them. This important area of church life needed attention among the churches of the denomination, and an organized approach to the problem was mandatory.

Another reason for establishing a program of church music is that music groups in public schools and communities, recordings, television, and radio are bringing about new understandings and appreciations of music with which churches must cope. In many churches, the children and youth are ahead of the adult leaders, both in music knowledge and in appreciation, and therefore are often disappointed with the type of music used in their churches.

While the Music Ministry must be organized in a church in order to accomplish its best work, it should be kept in mind that music is a part of every program of a church. It is at this point that understanding the philosophy of Southern Baptists' approach to its church music program is greatly needed.

The music program in a church can become an end in itself. It can call attention to itself and can enlist and train a group of performers who will leave the church impoverished in congregational singing. It is possible to devote so much attention to the higher forms of church music that the people in the pew whose music appreciation has not advanced to that extent are missed completely. Perhaps there are almost as many theories regarding church music today as there are churches. The church choir and the graded choirs are valuable assets to every church. However, if they make listeners rather than participants out of the congregation, choirs become a hindrance rather than a help.

The Music Ministry exists for every person in the church. It should improve music in all the church organizations and worship services and should lead every member of the church and its organizations to understand the appropriateness, the meaning, and the significance of church music.

The Music Ministry has basic tasks to perform. We shall examine carefully these tasks in order to have a clear understanding of them.

I. TEACH MUSIC

To teach music means to instruct in the fundamentals of music; to develop skills, understanding, and appreciation; and to offer music-learning opportunities to all persons. Such instruction involves an understanding of notation, rhythm, pitch, intervals, scales, and the structure of music. Discovery and development of technical skills for performance, how music is written and translating it into understanding, interpretation, and appreciation are also involved.

1. *To Choir Members*

The graded choir program includes all age groups from the Beginner music activity through the Adult choir. The method of teaching these age groups will vary, not only according to the age group, but also according to the previous instruction in music which members of the group have had.

Teaching music to Beginners should begin with simple rhythmic activities, such as clapping, jumping, or marching to music and beating time on rhythm instruments.

The meaning of music symbols and certain music terms may be taught to the children through music games. Beginner children can be taught to identify the treble and bass clefs, whole, half, quarter, and eighth notes, and the grand staff. They may also become familiar with the piano keyboard. Of course, all activities for Beginners must be very informal, which is the principal reason for referring to the Beginner group as a music activity rather than as a Beginner choir. Small children should never be put on exhibition. Their singing should be uninhibited, expressive of real enjoyment, and free from complications. If they sing for a church service, both the children and the congregation should be prepared in advance so that the children will not be on exhibition and the church members will receive the children properly.

Following the two years in the Beginner music activity, the Primary, Junior, Intermediate, Young People's, and Adult choirs provide additional learning opportunities for persons to become familiar with music theory, form, terms, choral techniques, and literature. The continued learning experiences will lead each choir member to sight-read music and to develop good tone quality. He thereby adds new understandings and appreciations to his total learning experiences in the church.

Teaching music in such a progressive manner will develop choir members who will sing correctly and will understand what they sing.

In churches which have not had a graded choir program, the church choir members must be taught the fundamentals of music which they missed as children. If the director or minister of music will recognize this need for instruction in music, he can begin his work where the choir members are and can improve their understanding of music and their quality of performance.

2. *To Song Leaders and Instrumentalists*

It is important for all departments of the church educational organizations to have competent musicians. Those who play pianos and lead music need basic instruction in the fundamentals of music and in applying their skills. Many department programs are ineffective because of inappropriate choices of music and the slipshod manner in which music is played or led. There should be a regular period of instruction for department musicians until they become proficient in their tasks and remain so.

3. *To the Congregation*

Many Baptist churches are impoverished because they sing only a few hymns and gospel songs. The request to sing something familiar is perhaps the greatest single handicap to learning new hymns. Another problem is finding a time to teach a congregation new music. It is very difficult to worship while learning a new hymn; consequently, in-

struction in music usually should come at some other time. Although music can be taught to a congregation, many who come for worship will resent the introduction of something new into the worship service.

Perhaps the best means of giving instruction in music is through the textbook studies of the Church Study Course. Most persons like music and enjoy singing. If courses are conducted in an interesting manner and are given good promotion, larger numbers of church members will learn music. The director of music or the minister of music should consider the congregation as a class and the hymnal as the textbook. He should become the best teacher possible.

II. TRAIN PERSONS TO LEAD, SING, AND PLAY MUSIC

Music is an exacting art. It must be sung and played as it is written. The text must be interpreted in keeping with the music which accompanies it. If those who sing or play develop their own tempo, or sing or play as they wish without regard for the musical score, they will prove to be a handicap to the church.

There are differences in teaching music and in training persons to lead, sing, and play music. Teaching music involves instruction in the recognition and understanding of musical symbols, terms, and forms, while training consists of practicing and rehearsing these symbols, terms, and forms until skills in recognition and utilization have been developed. Training involves participation until a person becomes skilful in the act.

The development of proper skills requires regular periods of rehearsal under trained leaders. A graded choir program should not be attempted until a church has adequate leaders to conduct it. Although a fully graded choir program is desirable, it is entirely possible that such a program must be developed over a period of years. Some churches are fortunate to have leaders who are skilled in working with the various age groups. Other churches are seriously handicapped by a lack of trained personnel. In a church where leadership has to be developed, the director of music or the

minister of music will perhaps need to work with potential leaders individually until each choir has adequate leadership. The same will also be true in the development of department musicians. In such instances, a regular schedule of practice can be established at the church so that those who are interested may practice on the piano or organ and may practice leading the singing. It is quite possible that a department pianist and song leader could rehearse together each week so as to be fully prepared for leading the music in their department the following Sunday.

Often songs which are to be used in various departments are indicated to the musicians at the weekly meetings of the organizations. Through such advance notice, adequate preparation may be made for Sunday meetings. It is as important for musicians to be skilled and prepared as it is for officers and teachers and other workers. Category 19 of the Church Study Course, Music Ministry Principles and Methods, contains excellent books which may be studied in classes or at home by those who are interested in developing skills in leading and playing music.

When a church has a full-time minister of music, it is his responsibility to guide in the enlistment and training of all department musicians for the educational organizations. In doing so, he will, of course, work with the minister of education and the heads of the departments involved.

While most of the training of singers may be achieved in the rehearsals of the various choirs, many ministers of music find it possible to conduct regular classes in voice and theory for choir members. In such classes, breath control, enunciation and pronunciation, diction, phrasing, sight-reading, theory, and vocal techniques are discussed and demonstrated. Such classes often achieve the best results by meeting once a week for a number of months. The training of ensembles and soloists also is a responsibility of the minister of music. These are scheduled for special rehearsals at times convenient to them and the minister of music. In some churches, the minister of music gives private voice instruction to certain singers. This coaching assures a higher quality

of soloists, as well as a better level of performance by the various members of the choirs and other singing groups.

III. LEAD PERSONS TO PARTICIPATE IN HYMN SINGING AND TO UNDERSTAND HYMNODY

Music and hymnody constitute the study program of the Music Ministry of a church. Although the hymnal is the basic textbook for the Music Ministry, music in many forms is available as additional curriculum materials.

The units of study produced by the Church Music Department of the Sunday School Board are among the finest prepared by any denomination. They are carefully planned as a part of the total curriculum materials of a Baptist church and are correlated with the Sunday school and Training Union lesson course materials.

Since music is a universal language, those who learn music are able to communicate with persons of other nationalities whose spoken language they may not understand. For this reason, music can become an increasingly effective instrument for world missions.

Familiar hymn tunes assist in developing fellowship among Christians around the world. Those who have attended sessions of the Baptist World Alliance find it interesting to hear such hymns as "Amazing Grace," "When I Survey the Wondrous Cross," and "Blessed Assurance, Jesus Is Mine" sung in many languages but to the same hymn tune. Even those who do not have a technical understanding of music gain much from singing. Music makes a major contribution to Christian family life. Music in the home is a major means of learning music.

Next to the Bible itself, the hymnal is perhaps the greatest storehouse of religious truth in print. It is true that some hymn writers have exercised poetic license in producing their literary compositions, and the texts of hymns do not always present the theological beliefs of Baptists. Certain hymn writers of other religious faiths have written texts which are not in keeping with Baptist belief and interpretation. Such hymns, however, have been carefully edited be-

fore being included in Baptist hymnals so as to express more accurately and definitely Baptist theological concepts. The hymnal contains such a treasury of religious poetry, as well as music, that it may be read daily with profit. For this reason a person may desire to buy his own copy. Since hymnody is a part of the religious heritage of Christianity, it should be known, understood, and appreciated by all church members.

What should be the content areas of the study program of the Music Ministry? All church members should be introduced to the music of the Old Testament. This would involve not only a study of the book of Psalms, which was the hymnbook of the Hebrew people, but also a study of other songs which appear in the Old Testament, such as the music used for the dedication of the Temple.

In the New Testament, such songs as Luke 1:46–55; 1:68–79; 2:14; and 2:29–32, which refer to the coming of Christ, should be studied. Included also should be the use of music pertaining to Christ's triumphal entry to Jerusalem, music at the Last Supper, and music in the book of Acts, the Epistles, and Revelation.

Other areas of study should be hymns of early Christendom to about the sixth century and Medieval Latin hymns. Martin Luther and German hymnody constitute an important area of study. Such pioneer English hymn writers as John Milton, John Bunyan, and Thomas Ken should be considered along with the hymns which they produced. Later English hymnody, American hymnody, and the gospel hymn also constitute areas of study which should be included in the study program of the Music Ministry.

IV. ASSIST THE CHURCH IN ITS FUNCTIONS

Music is a vital part of every phase of the life of a church. It is necessary to the effective functioning of a church.

1. *To Worship*

It has been stated earlier that the most important function of the church is worship. Yet in many instances it is

the most lightly regarded of all functions. If a church is to do Christ's work in the world, it must be composed of individuals who are rightly related to Christ and his spiritual power. This relationship comes through private and corporate worship.

Music is a means of worship. If one is singing with awareness and with intelligence, music will be expressive of many facets of the worship experience. Through music one may engage in praise, adoration, petition, intercession, confession, and repentance. The flights of imagination and feeling expressed through singing aid the worshiper to voice his feelings to God more clearly and more satisfactorily than in other ways. Music is in no sense a substitute for prayer or for the personal expression of the worshiper in his own words and thought patterns. However, it is a mistake to think of music in the worship service as being incidental, perfunctory, or something to be engaged in while latecomers are being seated, while the offering is being received, or while the church is being properly ventilated.

A service of worship would be poorer indeed without effective music. Music and religion have always gone together, and music and Christianity have been inseparable from the New Testament era to the present. Since congregational singing, instrumental numbers, and special music by choirs, ensembles, and soloists are given much time in a worship service, music should be recognized for what it is —a means of worship. All music should be carefully chosen in co-operation with the pastor to accomplish the purposes of the worship service. Music can be used to create a mood or atmosphere for worship. It may be used to call worshipers from their daily tasks to a new and vital relationship with God. Music may lead church members to dedicate their gifts to God, to be receptive to the reading of the Scriptures, and to unite their hearts in prayer. It may also be used as preparation to hear a sermon, as a part of the sermon, as an invitation to repentance, or as an invitation to join the church. Not to give music its rightful place is to deny church members one of their most important means of worship.

2. *To Proclaim*

Proclamation means the direct communication of the gospel to those in unbelief. A Christian may proclaim the gospel to a non-Christian. A teacher may proclaim the gospel to members of his class. A pastor may proclaim the gospel as he preaches.

It is in the latter connection that music plays its most vital role. All hymns and gospel songs which are true to the Bible may be used to assist in proclaiming the gospel. A survey of the topical index of a hymnal will indicate the types of hymns most usable in proclaiming the mighty acts of God through Christ. Such categories as assurance, atonement, baptism, the birth of Christ, the blood of Christ, the cross of Christ, the leadership of Christ, the love of Christ, the resurrection of Christ, the return of Christ, Christ as Saviour, eternal life, faith, the gospel, grace, heaven, and Holy Spirit indicate the range of music material which is available for proclaiming the gospel.

A survey of circumstances under which persons accepted Christ would indicate the influence of the invitation hymn in the making of these decisions. Who can measure the effect of such invitation hymns as "Almost Persuaded Now to Believe," "Christ Receiveth Sinful Men," "I Will Arise and Go to Jesus," "Jesus Is Tenderly Calling," "Just As I Am," "Only Trust Him," "Pass Me Not, O Gentle Saviour," "Softly and Tenderly," "My Soul in Sad Exile," "The Nail-scarred Hand," and "Ye Must Be Born Again"?

Christians bear a real witness through their singing. They sing of what Christ did to save them, and what he did to save all sinners. They sing of his death, burial, resurrection, and second coming. They proclaim his love, grace, and power to save. They express in song the glorious gospel and the joys of their own salvation. They testify through song.

Music is used in proclaiming the gospel not only in church worship services but also in departmental decision services. It can be used in street services, in open-air evangelistic meetings, and in homes. In each circumstance, it can serve

the same useful purpose in proclaiming what God has done for man through Jesus Christ.

3. *To Educate*

In addition to being used for worship in the several departments of the church educational organizations, church music plays a vital role in educating those who are members of these organizations.

Evidently much is learned from music, or else there would not be such widespread use of the singing commercial on radio and television. A catchy tune will sell a product which cannot be sold in any other way. Cigarette manufacturers and brewers of beer learned this fact long ago. Many nonsmokers and nondrinkers whistle or sing a tune they hear even though they may be opposed to the product the commercial is promoting. Concepts are conveyed when sung to catchy tunes. Ideas are grasped more readily when the imagination and emotions are involved. Music stirs the imagination and appeals to the emotions.

Repetition is important in learning. One cannot repeat an expression often in a spoken message without its becoming monotonous. However, the idea may be repeated again and again when it is set to music. There is more toleration and acceptance of the same idea when it is sung repeatedly than when the same idea is spoken frequently. The association of ideas is involved where the tune and words are related. A tune which is easy to remember will aid in the recall of the meaning of the words used with it. If the tune is attractive, the words will be remembered more readily. It would be interesting to know how many theological concepts have been impressed upon people through music.

The Church Music Department of the Sunday School Board is further fulfilling its educational mission by working with the Sunday School, Training Union, Student, Church Administration, and Family Life departments of the Sunday School Board in the selection and utilization of the Hymn of the Month. These departments assist the Church Music

Department in motivating Baptist church members to learn a new hymn each month of the year.

The Church Music Department is working with these same departments in correlating music with the education curriculum in such a way as to make music a vital part of the content of all courses of study. Through these various media, music can fulfil its rightful place in the educational function of the church.

4. *To Minister*

There are various ways in which music may be used in the ministry of a church. Music makes a definite contribution to weddings and other social occasions. What would a wedding be without music? Musical preludes, vocal music, wedding marches, and music during a wedding ceremony add beauty, reverence, and solemnity to the occasion.

Music at banquets and other social gatherings of the church give life, vitality, and charm to the meetings.

Lighter types of music at fellowship gatherings and informal meetings lead young people and their workers to respond with enthusiasm and joy to such occasions.

Music has a real ministry in the homes of church members. Hymn singing in family worship, singing grace at meals, instruction in developing music appreciation and skills in children and parents, guidance in the selection of good recordings, music on radio and television, community music projects—all have a place in the ministry of music in the church as it relates to the home.

On its more serious side, music at funerals gives comfort, hope, and trust to those who sorrow. Music, more than any other factor except the reading of the Bible and prayer, seems to speak of God's love, care, and grace in time of separation and sorrow. When D day came in France, the popular radio programs on that day turned from popular music to the great church hymns and musical classics. On a day when lives were being lost for freedom, popular music was out of place. Music is a vital means of ministering to the needs of church members.

V. Provide and Interpret Information Regarding the Work of the Church and the Denomination

The Music Ministry can be used by the church to interpret important information to each of its members. In this way each choir member and each instrumentalist can be properly related to the total life and work of the church. It has been found by most ministers of music that church members who are faithful to the various services and activities of the churches make the best choir members. Doubtless, this is true because these church members are better informed and are, therefore, more devoted to all functions of their churches.

Today the Music Ministry is growing rapidly and as an organization may be found in approximately one half of all Southern Baptist churches. It is becoming a significant denominational force fully committed to use by the churches and the denomination.

The Church Music Department of the Sunday School Board is a channel department similar to the Sunday School and Training Union. This department does not publish as many periodicals as the Sunday School and Training Union departments, but the materials it publishes reach thousands of persons who are engaged in the music program of the churches. Since music is a part of the total work of a church, its program is related to other church programs. However, since the Music Ministry is organized to achieve the objectives of the music program of the churches, it, too, is a channel of communication for the churches and denomination.

Hence, those who plan and suggest program materials in the Church Music Department of the Sunday School Board are constantly seeking to use the opportunities they have for channeling other Southern Baptist Convention programs to those engaged in the Music Ministry of the churches.

The Church Musician carries articles of general interest to its readers regarding the work of Southern Baptists. The Church Music Department co-operates fully with the

Church Administration Department in interpreting to ministers of music their relationships to the church council. The Church Music Department works with the Church Recreation Department of the Sunday School Board in developing plans for the social and recreational life of the members of the Music Ministry. It co-operates with the Church Library Department of the Sunday School Board in the use of the facilities of the library for reading and for the use of audio-visuals. It works in close co-operation with the Church Architecture Department in planning for the needs of the Music Ministry in church buildings. The Church Music Department also co-operates with the leader of the vocational guidance program in building proper vocational emphasis into its materials. Such co-operation is followed carefully with regard to other Convention programs. These areas of co-operation make possible the interpretation of valuable denominational information to those enrolled in the Music Ministry of the churches.

CHAPTER 9

I. LIBRARY SERVICE
   1. Procure Materials
   2. Care for Materials
   3. Encourage the Use of Materials
   4. Circulate Materials

II. AUDIO-VISUAL SERVICE
   1. Program the Use of Audio-Visuals
   2. Train Leaders to Use Audio-Visual Materials and Equipment

III. RECREATION SERVICE
   1. Determine Recreation Capacities of the Members
   2. Plan a Program of Recreation Activities
   3. Assist Organizations in Recreation Activities

9

The Task of
OTHER CHURCH PROGRAMS

CERTAIN PROGRAMS of the church are significant because of the service they render to church members and organizations. For this reason they are often referred to as program services, that is, they serve other programs. The services which they provide greatly enrich the life and work of a congregation and make a positive contribution to church members.

I. LIBRARY SERVICE

Reading has been a practice of Christians throughout the centuries. The New Testament church members gave much attention to the reading of the Scriptures. The Reformation in Europe sprang from an emphasis on the necessity of every person's reading and interpreting the Bible for himself. Our Baptist forefathers, though often lacking formal education, were great believers in Bible reading and in reading other great literature of their day. Christ said, "Ye shall know the truth, and the truth shall make you free." Now, as then, it is the searching mind that finds the truth. Many resources provide opportunity for Christians to search the minds and hearts of others and to experience with them a search for truth as God has revealed it.

Baptists discovered long ago that the effectiveness of a spiritual democracy depends upon an intelligent and in-

formed constituency. This discovery led them to seek information and knowledge for Christian action from every source. Today the search for truth and knowledge continues. In all Baptist churches, there is a continual need for resource materials to help individual members and to aid and supplement the organizational activities. Individually owned materials are often costly, difficult to obtain, and hard to store for future use. Therefore, it is logical for a church to have a library.

Today's concept of a church library is that of a resource center where many types of materials are housed. In this center are printed materials, including books, pamphlets, tracts, and clippings. There are also audio-visual materials such as slides, filmstrips, maps, recordings, and pictures. Audio-visual equipment and materials for interest centers are other resources which may be found in a library.

The library service is a church's means of procuring materials, caring for them, encouraging their use, and circulating them to the people of the church.

1. *Procure Materials*

Each piece of church literature carries recommended titles and lists of materials suggested for use in the work of organizations and by individuals. While all this material is worthwhile and helpful, most churches find it necessary to select what is the most helpful for them. In addition to recommendations found in church literature, materials are advertised in newspapers and displayed attractively in stores, and thus made appealing to possible purchasers.

What then should be bought? The church library service seeks to insure the best use of money in the purchase of materials needed by the church members and leaders. The library should contain a selection of worthwhile materials geared to meet the needs and requests of its borrowers. A balance of materials for all age groups should be included in the library. These materials should be of high quality. The library, through its materials, seeks to minister to the whole of life. The physical, mental, social, and spiritual needs of

persons should be kept in mind. Books and audio-visual items should be purchased to help each person in the church, regardless of age, achieve his mental and spiritual potential.

The content of church literature is always limited because of space. Many times additional help is needed for enrichment, enlightment, or illustration. Teachers may desire expository helps in studying their Bibles. Program leaders need assistance in preparing meaningful presentations and interpretations of topics. Pastors seek sources of new help as they counsel and guide the lost and the perplexed. The library service is the ideal source of material to meet these and other requirements.

Each item to be placed in the library should be evaluated according to the standards of selection determined by the church. This evaluation should be in the areas of content, usefulness, and physical make-up. In content, all materials should be examined to see that the material is accurate. Facts, Scripture interpretations, and doctrinal views should be authentic and sound. Certain types of audio-visual aids and illustrations in books may need special attention. This is especially true in materials for children. Extreme care and caution should be exercised to assure that misconceptions are not created. Material placed in a library should be constructive in influence, morally uplifting, educationally sound, well prepared, and up to date.

Materials should normally have a potential of continued use rather than a single use value. Care should be taken to see that materials are not procured, used one time, and never touched again.

In considering physical make-up, materials of a good quality, attractive, and durable should be chosen. Visual aid equipment should be selected with special care and examination relative to quality, use, and price.

The librarian, library staff, and church leaders are responsible for the selection of library materials. Certain selections will result from requests by program leaders based upon their budgets. Other general, or nonprogram, materials

will be selected by the library staff. All church members, however, should feel free to make suggestions and recommendations for purchases. In the selection of audio-visual materials, the audio-visual aids librarian will work closely with the superintendent of audio-visual aids in the Sunday school, the director of audio-visual aids in the Training Union, and the audio-visual officers in the other organizations.

In many churches without libraries, a large number of materials which should go in a library can often be found. A library service could be started with the simple actions of a church vote to do so, election of a librarian and library staff, gathering the materials into one approved location, and establishment of library hours.

The church is responsible for financing its library. Although gifts and memorial items should be gratefully received, the best plan for financing a library is through the church budget.

Libraries, like churches, will vary in size and content. A separate room, centrally located, is the ideal location for a library. However, many libraries are begun in class rooms, corridors, or in mobile shelving units.

2. *Care for Materials*

The library not only provides materials for use but also cares for them in order that fullest value will be received from each item purchased. A church may spend hundreds of dollars needlessly purchasing materials over and over again. Maps of the Holy Land, Bible study helps, and books about missionaries are examples of materials that can be used many times over. A search in a church may uncover a print of Hunt's *The Light of the World,* a "lost" filmstrip projector, or a set of teaching filmstrips. Persons now requesting one of these items would probably be informed that the church did not possess it. In many cases, materials are soon damaged, and thus discarded. The library provides for the location of lost materials and the repair of damaged ones.

The library, through a systematic process, prepares ma-

terial for use. The steps necessary in readying an item for use are vital to the life of the item and its use by the borrower. In the processing of materials, conditioning care is given some items prior to use or repair to items damaged in use. A simple, quick placement of tape on a torn page can make a book available for many additional users.

Maintaining audio-visual materials and equipment requires skill and vigilance. For the equipment to be of value, it must be kept in satisfactory operating condition. The library staff should include someone especially trained for this service.

The preparation of the card catalog is essential in caring adequately for materials. Maintaining an up-to-date catalog also insures that borrowers may know about and locate materials. This is an important action through which a library staff serves its church.

By keeping up with the materials that are in use, the library service cares for its resources. A systematic method of overdue notices, telephone calls, and personal contacts should remind borrowers of their need to return materials and equipment. Small fines charged on overdue items may assist in getting materials back.

3. *Encourage the Use of Materials*

A library may be in the best location possible and may contain many worthwhile materials; but if materials are not used, the library will be of little value. Therefore, the library staff and the leadership of the church should encourage the use of the materials at every opportunity. They should inform the church membership of the materials and services of the library. Such encouragement and information will increase the use of the materials and create good will for the library. Plans should include teaching church leaders the value of resource materials and the methods of using them effectively.

Many Baptist churches have failed to capitalize on the use of audio-visual materials because of a lack of information concerning them or a misconception of their pur-

pose. The library staff can demonstrate the value of such properly used materials and help erase the idea that a film is used when nothing else has been planned.

Special promotion such as reading clubs and library emphasis weeks can help to establish in the minds of the church people the place and purpose of the library. Posters, bulletin boards, displays, announcements, and lists of materials related to topics should be employed to encourage use of resources.

The library staff should have primary responsibility for promoting the use of the resource materials. However, all borrowers and church workers should have opportunity to encourage use of resources by those with whom they come in contact.

4. *Circulate Materials*

Perhaps the most important work of the library service is the operation of the library. Specifically designated library hours should be scheduled, publicized, and maintained. These hours should be determined by the needs of the church members. A member of the library staff should be on duty at each of the designated times. The staff members should assist borrowers in finding materials and by making suggestions or recommendations when appropriate.

Reservations for the use of audio-visual materials and equipment should be made in advance by the library staff. Advance scheduling assures the borrower that he will have items when he needs them. This eliminates the conflict and unhappiness which comes when at the last minute a person finds that all equipment is in use. Audio-visual materials should be picked up at the library and returned immediately following their use.

Many libraries circulate materials not only from the library room but also from centers outside the library. Designated locations in other buildings can serve to make resource materials available to a larger number of persons. Selected material can also be taken to departments, classes, unions, and other organizational meetings. The use of materials

from the library may be greatly increased and of special help if circulated to children's groups for use in connection with their units of study.

Circulation records should be kept in order that reports can be made as to what is being used and where. This information can be important in improving the circulation of a church's library materials.

II. AUDIO-VISUAL SERVICE

The present generation of Baptists is the first to enjoy the benefits of audio-visuals. The identification of all films with Hollywood led Baptist churches to reject the use of audio-visuals for many years. More recently, however, congregations have realized that audio-visuals can motivate persons in decision-making.

Since Christianity is primarily a life of decision-making for God, this new discovery has real significance. Churches can strengthen their challenge to Christlike living through the appropriate use of audio-visuals.

Audio-visuals can also improve learning. Churches have discovered that audio-visuals can assist persons to learn more rapidly, to learn better, and to learn more. Because audio-visuals serve all the programs of the church, the congregation should assign the following responsibilities.

1. *Program the Use of Audio-Visuals*

Many Baptist churches now own audio-visual equipment, films, and filmstrips and enjoy the results that come from their use. In churches where audio-visual materials are available, many leaders have not learned how to use them to improve their work. A church is obligated to plan with its leaders the use of audio-visuals to enrich their work. This is the beginning place for an audio-visual service.

Many churches believe that the purchase of a piece of equipment or of a particular filmstrip is all that is needed. Other churches report that investments in equipment and materials are a waste of resources unless church leaders understand the value and purpose of audio-visuals.

Many wonderful films and filmstrips have been produced in recent years. Some are of value in assisting teachers in their task of instruction. Others have been prepared to dramatize life situations and to challenge persons to commit themselves to the work of Christ. Few church leaders are acquainted with the vast amount of material available. The preparation of bibliographies of these resources is a task of persons assigned the responsibility for audio-visuals in the church. Bibliographies should list materials that are available and should give suggestions as to when these materials may be used. Most educational organizations in large churches should have an officer whose sole responsibility is this task. Helpful assistance in preparing bibliographies is provided through most of the monthly magazines.

2. *Train Leaders to Use Audio-Visual Materials and Equipment*

One of the major handicaps to more extensive and better use of audio-visuals is the lack of skill in operating motion-picture and filmstrip projectors. A real service is rendered by the audio-visual leaders when they train church leaders in the proper and effective use of audio-visual equipment. With the great turnover of leadership in Baptist churches, training of church leaders should be a constant activity. Training activities should help church leaders make the best use of all audio-visual equipment the church provides.

Training in the proper selection and use of audio-visual materials is perhaps more important than training in the use of equipment. The properly planned use of audio-visuals to enrich and supplement the programs of a church is still a rare thing in thousands of Southern Baptist churches. Responsibility here as in all areas of actions belongs to the church leaders. Leadership training is the surest way to correct this situation.

III. RECREATION SERVICE

A discussion in chapter 4 pointed out that a new concept of the person is needed. The time has come to give more

attention to the mental and physical needs of the individual. Christ gave attention to the physical needs of himself, as well as of other persons. Consider how often he pushed through the multitudes to make his way into the mountains or into the desert or to a boat so that he might have time alone. It is impossible to prove from the Scriptures that Jesus spent much time in recreation, but we do know from his ministry that he was concerned with the bodies of men. He cured the sick, healed the lame, gave sight to the blind, and sympathized with the tired.

The word "recreation" is best understood when spelled "re-creation." In addition to renewing their spirits, Baptists need to give attention to conserving this renewal of spirit and to renewing the strength and life of their bodies as well. They need to discover new ways to express themselves through their minds and bodies. The recreation service of a church can provide ways for persons to relax from the strain of daily work and refresh themselves through re-creative leisure-time activity.

Of the millions of Southern Baptists, a large percentage of the adults live in the city and work in offices. Their only exercise during the day is the walking which they do within the building or on their way to and from lunch. By the time they arrive home in the evening, it is too dark for them to spend much time outdoors. Under such conditions, it is no wonder that emotional tension is a characteristic of our age. Physical exercise has always provided a release for emotional tension, as well as refreshment for the staleness that results from inactivity. As our society becomes more urbanized, churches must give more consideration to a ministry by which church members may release their pent-up emotions in a healthy manner.

Social graces and habits are harmonious with Christian teachings. More and more in our society the individual is being overlooked. Common courtesies of a few years ago are almost ignored today. Surely churches along with families have the responsibility to develop in their members those graces which will make them attractive to the world.

Beauty is of God. The highest experiences that a man can have are always closely related to his idea of beauty. Church recreation should provide means by which individual persons can become beautiful in their actions, in their habits, and in their expressions.

Recreation should not only build stronger bodies and give new avenues of expression; it should also provide another means of Christian fellowship. As churches grow in size and as time schedules become more exacting, church members spend less and less time in relaxed fellowship with one another. They hurry to church, sit in classes or unions, hurry to worship services, and then hurry home. Congregations need opportunities when they can come together in relaxed fellowship. Out of such experiences friendships develop. Such friendship is vital to the ongoing mission of a church.

1. *Determine the Recreation Capacities of the Members*

There are many forms of recreation. The interests and capacities of each person determine the recreation activities which he will most enjoy. The geographical location and economic condition of a church will influence the recreation its members will appreciate. Those charged with responsibility for providing recreation activities and opportunities need to analyze the membership and to determine the activities which are most likely to appeal to their church. This may require a survey to discover what the church members do. Evaluation of recreation activities and opportunities will indicate what contribution recreation is making in harmony with the objectives of the church.

2. *Plan a Program of Recreation Activities*

Since most church organizations make recreation activities an integral part of their programing, any recreation program of the church needs to be developed co-operatively with all church leaders. Consideration should be given to what recreation activities each organization will provide church members. Having determined this, the responsible recreation personnel should plan a well-balanced and com-

prehensive program of recreation. This planning may be done best through the church council. Such a program should supplement and strengthen those planned by the individual organizations. This expansion should take into account the recreation needs of the congregation as a whole. So far, churches have majored on recreation programs for teen-agers and older adults. The time has come when the recreation program should be planned to meet the needs of the whole congregation including the children.

3. *Assist Organizations in Recreation Activities*

The recreation service of a church can be of particular assistance to the other church organizations. Quite often the leaders in Sunday school, Training Union, and other organizations have not learned how to plan recreation opportunities. Many churches have established committees of selected individuals who have had training in planning recreation. Other churches employ recreation directors who advise the church organizations through a church recreation committee on their recreation activities. The recreation leaders can expand their ministry by training leaders in church organizations in the use of recreation as a means of more effective education.

Church recreation leaders may assist in planning of recreation activities to be sponsored by the organizations. If special skill or knowledge is required for a particular recreation activity, those charged by the church to give specific recreation service may provide this skill or knowledge.

How can recreation contribute to the church's functions of worship, proclamation, education, and ministry? This is a question every congregation must answer as it considers expanding its recreation program. As in the other church programs, objectives should be clearly stated to show their relationship to the primary functions of the church. Leadership, finances, and facilities of the church should be provided on the basis of the contribution recreation will make to the total church program.

CHAPTER 10

The Means for

CONDUCTING THE PROGRAMS OF A CHURCH

OBJECTIVES should set forth the ends which a congregation hopes to achieve. The programs which it authorizes and carries on are the planned actions for achieving these objectives. Actions may occur spontaneously. However, if a church desires a particular action to take place regularly and effectively, certain steps must be taken to guarantee this. The following means are usually required for carrying on the basic activities of a church.

I. ORGANIZATION

Organization is the plan by which a group of people work together. Organization is man-made, but God has used it for accomplishing many wonderful things. The church, which Christ established, is an organization and it has organizations. The organization of a Baptist church represents the way the congregation has decided to delegate responsibility for carrying out its functions, programs, and tasks.

Organization is not an end in itself; nor are the several organizations of a church. They are means to an end. If an organization is not performing properly its assigned responsibilities, a careful evaluation needs to be made; and proper action should be taken. An organization should not

131

be established if it is not needed; nor should it be permitted to continue if it is not making a significant contribution to the basic objectives of the church. Baptist churches need to give careful consideration before multiplying the number of organizations.

Not all organizations are of equal importance to the life of the church. When the congregation is asked to provide leaders, finances, and facilities for organizations, it needs to do so on the basis of the contribution the organizations will make to the total life and work of the church.

Constituting an organization or organizations is the responsibility of each Baptist church. Establishing, altering, or discontinuing an organization is likewise the responsibility of the congregation as a whole. The responsibility for making recommendations concerning organizational changes can and should, however, be assigned to the selected leaders in the church.

II. LEADERSHIP

Attention has already been given to the place and purpose of leadership in a Baptist church. Consideration needs to be given, also, to the necessity of providing adequate leadership. People do not automatically become leaders upon selection by a church. A leader is one who understands the purposes of the organization he serves. He understands the responsibilities which have been assigned to him, and he is skilled in performing the assigned responsibilities. He understands the effect his leadership or lack of leadership has on the success of his organization's work. A leader must understand when he is to take the initiative in leading.

We have already noted a number of positions which require leaders in a Baptist church. There are many more. Teachers, department superintendents and directors, class and union officers, secretaries, song leaders, and pianists are typical.

To fill these positions a church must:

(1) discover potential leaders
(2) recruit potential leaders

(3) train them for their tasks
(4) enlist them in specific offices
(5) assist them in getting adjusted to their work
(6) help them develop their full potential
(7) guide them properly as they serve

A congregation must realize that when it authorizes a program and establishes an organization, it is making a commitment to provide leaders for the organization. These leaders must come from the congregation. The lack of experienced leaders should not keep a congregation from establishing organization, for leaders can be discovered, enlisted, and trained. Becoming a leader should be the goal of every church member. This is sound doctrine when one understands leadership as the task of calling persons away from self-centeredness, from the less important to the more important; from segmented living to the wholeness of life. A church's call to a place of leadership should be a call to a better way of life.

III. CURRICULUM AND LEADERSHIP MATERIALS

Curriculum and leadership materials have always been appreciated by Baptists. Although they are committed first to studying the Bible, they have recognized the need for materials to guide their learning experiences and to give instruction in specialized areas of leadership and administration. A problem for most churches results when members take materials for granted.

A study of most church budgets will reveal that a sizeable amount of their financial resources is invested in church literature. Such an investment warrants the best use of purchased materials. In some churches this will mean a better system for distributing periodicals. It will also mean better use of materials.

Baptist churches could well afford to spend several weeks training their members in the proper use of the materials provided. Such instruction is necessary because materials are produced for specific purposes closely related to the objectives of the church. Proper use, based upon the purposes,

should result in the achievement of the objectives the church had in purchasing the materials.

Many curriculum materials are produced by denominational agencies for use by churches. Responsible church leaders will select what best fits the needs of their church before they order the quantity needed.

The congregation is responsible for providing enough of the best materials available; leaders are responsible for seeing that the materials are available at the right moment; the congregation is responsible for using the materials in the right way.

IV. SCHEDULES

Scheduling is a major consideration for Baptist churches. It is one of the most complex problems a congregation faces. Factors that influence the number of activities scheduled and the time for these activities include the objectives of the church, its size and location, number and ages of members, community activities which the church has a responsibility to support, the congregation's family life, and the physical condition of the members. Most Baptist churches think in terms of decreasing the number and length of activities. They may be right, or it is possible that some churches need to increase the number and length of activities.

Setting the time for Sunday school, Training Union, worship services, or other activities of the church is the task of the congregation and its leaders working through the church council. Traditional approaches to scheduling are valid only if they prove to be adequate. A congregation should not be hesitant to change schedules if the church will benefit from change.

V. PROPERTY AND BUILDINGS

Baptist churches have invested tremendous sums in property and buildings. As churches have increased in size and in their programing, more property and buildings have been required. Space is a contributing factor to the growth or lack of growth in a church. Buildings affect the quality

of results achieved through the programs of the church. New buildings should be built with the expectation that the church will provide an enlarged and improved ministry to the congregation and the community.

The purposes for which a building is to be constructed and the expected cost for constructing a new building should be evaluated in terms of the basic objectives of the church. Congregations should take a closer look at the way their buildings are being used. Many, worth hundreds of thousands of dollars, are being used only two or three hours a week. Is it possible that churches could find additional uses for these resources?

Baptists have given too little attention to kindergartens and special weekday classes for their members. Many members of the congregation and other persons in the community find it impossible to attend Sunday school or other activities on Sunday. Is it possible that Sunday schools should operate some departments as Monday schools or Thursday schools? Is it possible that special sessions of informal church groups might be held to discuss current issues, to do special studies, or to pray? Church buildings can contribute to the beauty of the community and can call the passer-by to God, but their primary value comes from use in accomplishing specific objectives through specifically planned activities.

VI. SUPPLIES AND EQUIPMENT

A decision to establish a program or organization is a commitment to spend the financial resources of the church for the purchase of proper supplies and equipment.

It is amazing how many different items are used by churches in their work. Office supplies and cleaning aids are obviously needed. Hundreds of dollars are spent on items such as crayons, paper, chalk, or maps. Such purchases are valid if churches desire their programs to be rich, interesting, and challenging. The purchase of supplies should not be limited to the point that the work of a church is hindered. But a congregation has the right to expect that

only the proper supplies and equipment be purchased and that they be properly used.

Requests for supplies and equipment should be made according to the policies and procedures of a church. Many churches require leaders to budget in advance according to expected needs. For example, Nursery departments may be asked to indicate the expense for juice or other refreshments to be served children each week, or a department may be requested to indicate the number of new chalkboards or maps needed for the coming year. Such budgeting may not always be possible, but when used, it emphasizes the fact that supplies and equipment are to be purchased wisely.

Church leaders who have requested and received supplies and equipment have an obligation to the congregation to safeguard these investments. In almost every church one can find examples of misuse, waste, and destruction of supplies and equipment. Responsible leaders will keep such loss to a minimum.

VII. FINANCES

A congregation should know how it is spending its money. It should know how the association, state, and Southern Baptist Convention use money which a church provides.

Few churches, however, have developed the procedure of budgeting their finances according to the programs which will spend the money. Such a method of budgeting provides helpful insights into the church's actual use of its financial resources. The congregation can plan better to achieve major goals when budgets reflect adequate financial support. Areas of work left undone can be easily spotted. Activities that prove to be too costly can be controlled.

A congregation needs to know how it is spending dollars in getting the work of the church done through its established programs and organizations. For instance, what does it cost to operate the Sunday school in a church? How much did the church spend on recreation last year? What does the WMU program require? These and other questions should be of interest to every member of a congregation.

Another way to ask these questions is this: How much money did the Sunday school need to carry on a full program? How much was the church unable to do in ministering to people last year because of lack of money? Many Baptist churches have the habit of first asking members of the congregation what they will give. Congregations should decide what God wants them to do, determine the finances required to do this, and then under the direction of the Lord seek to provide the financial resources needed to carry out the program.

Financial reports are important. Programs in a church do not need or deserve equal amounts of money. The congregation is responsible for seeing that each program receives its proper share of the financial resources of a church and that the money is used properly. Budgets and budget reports should reflect to the congregation whether its instructions are being carried out. The money a church receives is important, but it is only a means to an end. Church leaders are responsible for turning the financial resources into spiritual ministries. Economy should be exercised in this process, but expenditures should be made when spiritual dividends will result.

VIII. ADMINISTRATIVE CONTROLS

The technical sounding term "administrative controls" has a simple meaning. Administrative controls are the means by which the congregation makes certain that its leaders are acting according to its wishes. The budget, for example, is such a control. A certain amount of money is approved in the budget for use by a program for specific actions. The budget report is an administrative control that informs the congregation whether proper use was made of the money authorized.

Another administrative control is the established procedure for making purchases. In some churches one person is authorized by the congregation to purchase all the equipment and supplies. Such a process gives the congregation control over the manner of purchasing. Another control is

the election of all church officers. Program leaders do not choose anyone for a place of leadership. Through election the congregation makes certain that the individual elected is properly qualified.

A congregation may use any number of administrative controls in the conduct of its affairs. However, the controls should not be so numerous that the elected leaders cannot take initiative or make decisions without the sanction of the congregation. Neither should the congregation feel that it is reflecting lack of confidence in its leaders to insist on some controls. In fact, the wise leader will appreciate some administrative controls because they relieve him of making some decisions. Or they may relieve him of certain responsibilities for which he should not be accountable. A church desiring guidance in establishing administrative controls will find help in the Church Administration Department materials provided by the Sunday School Board and in the Church Study Course books prepared as guides in setting up the church organizations.

IX. CHURCH-HOME CO-OPERATION

Church-home co-operation should not be considered as a means only. Families, like persons, are ends in themselves; they are not to be manipulated or used as tools at the discretion of the church. Nevertheless, a church in co-operating with its homes provides marvelous assistance in achieving church objectives. Some of these objectives will be achieved as the Christian family ministers to each of its members. Other objectives will be achieved as the church ministers to the family. Church members need to see the comprehensiveness of the church-home relationship.

Responsibility for the church's ministry to the family is shared by all the officers and organizations of the church. Much of the ministry is an integral part of the educational program and other activities which the church sponsors. Perhaps a consideration of the full ministry to its families would establish this fact best. The following suggested ob-

jectives are one way a congregation could state its total
family ministry:

Provide pastoral care for families
Educate persons for Christian marriage and family living
Establish a program of church-home co-operation
Build resources for family living
Minister, as a congregation, to the families of the church

Four of these objectives have been discussed or implied
in discussions of preceding chapters. The work of the pastor
and the deacons, the selection and use of the proper curriculum materials, and the basic programs of a church should
give a broad base to the church's family ministry.

Church-home co-operation is a conscious recognition and
agreement between the congregation and its families to hold
in common certain objectives and tasks in growing Christian
lives.

The planned program now consists of such activities as
parents encouraging children to read their Bibles daily, conducting family worship, using materials furnished by the
church, such as *Living with Children, Every Day with Pri-
maries,* and *Every Day with Beginners. Home Life* offers
helps for parents to use in a more direct teaching ministry
to their children. Some congregations have made more comprehensive plans than these; others have not used properly
the resources already available.

Churches must depend more and more upon responsible
Christian families to achieve the objectives Christ gave. As
cities grow and churches enlarge, there is the possibility
that it will be more difficult to give personal attention to the
individual church member. Churches that plan ahead and
plan well can offset the shortcomings of their own programing through sharing with families Christ's concern for
the individual person. This is truly a common task; for
families, like churches, have found their true meaning of
existence when they can say with Christ, "I am come that

they might have life, and that they might have it more abundantly" (John 10:10).

It is hoped that this study has established the fact that a church organized and functioning according to New Testament examples is both a theocracy and a democracy. It has basic tasks to perform and must always center its energies and full resources on them if it is to be a church. Each church must understand its functions, establish worthwhile objectives, plan its programs, and organize and conduct its work to achieve its objectives. In so doing, it will honor Christ and will contribute to the progress of his work in the world.

SUGGESTIONS FOR THE TEACHER

THE STUDY of this book can lead a church to increase greatly its effectiveness in the service of Christ. If you, the teacher, plan adequately, the study can become a great spiritual experience for those who participate. Study of the Bible, particularly those portions which are quoted or referred to in the book, and prayer are the essential starting place in making preparation to teach the book.

CHAPTER 1

Use the Bible in studying the material in this chapter. Lead the class to participate by locating, reading, and discussing the Scripture passages which are referred to in the chapter. Provide time, use a concordance, and look for additional references concerning the four functions of the church.

CHAPTER 2

Prior to the first session, ask several persons to study other books and make a brief report about the Southern Baptist position on congregational government. Start the discussion of chapter 2 with these reports.

Lead your class members to write a statement of objectives for your church.

CHAPTER 3

Ask the pastor to list on the chalkboard, and discuss, the phases of his pastoral ministry.

Present a skit showing the church council at work. Encourage members to react to the method and procedure of the council meeting.

Let the group participate in a make-believe church business meeting. Select a moderator, a clerk, and an item of business to be presented. Evaluate the business session.

Chapter 4

Provide a check sheet for each member of the group to use in evaluating the work of his Sunday school in worship, outreach, witness, and personal ministries. Lead them to give reasons for their answers.

Provide the record of the number of baptisms annually during the past five years. Study the trend in relation to the Sunday school enrolment during the same five years. Discuss the relationship.

Chapter 5

Guide members of the class in listing what they would do in performing the functions of a church. List specific skills required to carry out these actions. Discuss the assistance being given by the church's Training Union in developing these skills.

Gather information regarding the number of new leaders required by the church during the past three years. Discuss the meaning of this information to the Training Union's task of discovering, recruiting, and giving general training to potential leaders.

Chapter 6

Lead the group to list a specific mission service which their church may perform in the community, such as sharing food and clothing with the needy or visiting sick persons. Discuss the effect of such service on the church's witness to the community.

Chapter 7

Name recent events around the world that have an influence on Southern Baptist mission work. Suggest that the group list information regarding the event and the place where it happened. Discuss how the Brotherhood could supply such information regularly to its members.

Chapter 8

Supply each member of the class with a hymnal used by the church. Lead the members to find various sections of the hymnal and to discuss their purpose. Use the hymnal in discussing the material in the chapter.

CHAPTER 9

Gather and present records concerning the use of books and audio-visuals in the church during the past three years. Encourage members of the class to share the results of using audio-visuals and books from the church library.

CHAPTER 10

Make available to class members copies of the periodicals used in the various church organizations. Lead members of the group who use these periodicals to comment on their value.

Provide copies of the last church budget report. Let members discuss the meaning of the headings and the relative importance of the various expenditures.

Provide a sample of each periodical or leaflet being sent regularly to the home. Use the group to study and report the content of the various pieces.

FOR REVIEW AND WRITTEN WORK

CHAPTER 1
1. Discuss briefly the nature of a church.
2. List and define four basic functions of a church.

CHAPTER 2
3. Name six responsibilities of the congregation.
4. Discuss the reasons why a church should set objectives.
5. What do the terms "program," "program services," and "administrative services" mean?

CHAPTER 3
6. Why is administration a ministry?
7. What led to the choosing of the first deacons? What were they ordained to do?
8. Why should church leaders regularly recommend and report to the congregation?
9. Discuss ways that church business meetings can become more meaningful to the entire congregation.
10. What are the values of a church council?

CHAPTER 4
11. Why is teaching the biblical revelation such an important task of the Sunday school?
12. Why is the Sunday school the church's best agency for outreach?
13. What does "to witness" mean?
14. How does the Sunday school provide information for the church and the denomination?

CHAPTER 5
15. Name the study programs of the Training Union.
16. What are the objectives of the new church member orientation program?

17. What is meant by "to train" church members?
18. What is the difference in giving general training and specific training to church leaders?

CHAPTER 6

19. Name the tasks of Woman's Missionary Union.
20. Discuss the scope of the task of teaching the course of Christian missions. What is the relationship of study and prayer in missionary education?
21. What special projects does Woman's Missionary Union conduct for the church?

CHAPTER 7

22. What is meant by the words "missions" and "missionary education"?
23. Name the three tasks of the Brotherhood.
24. What missions projects does the Brotherhood provide for men?

CHAPTER 8

25. What is the Music Ministry? What requirements does a church have to meet in order to have a Music Ministry?
26. Discuss briefly how the Music Ministry assists the church to worship, to proclaim, to educate, and to minister.
27. What educational functions does the Music Ministry perform for the church?

CHAPTER 9

28. What are the purposes of the library service?
29. How can churches improve their work by using audio-visuals?
30. Discuss briefly the spiritual ministry of a church through the recreation service.

CHAPTER 10

31. Why is organization necessary in a church?
32. Name seven actions a church should take in providing leaders.
33. Discuss briefly the significance of church-home co-operation.

GLOSSARY

Administration—To lead people as a group to achieve spiritual goals.

Administrative control—The means by which the congregation makes certain that its leaders are acting according to its wishes.

Administrative service—A necessary continuing activity that exists to serve those who lead and guide the work of the church.

Channel organization—A Southern Baptist Convention organization which discovers, develops, and interprets its own program, but also interprets through its materials and programs the work of other Southern Baptist Convention boards, agencies, and institutions.

Conduct—To carry out according to plan actions or activities which have been developed.

Constitution—The congregation's formal statement of what it is and how it operates.

Content area—The material selected for presentation on a specific subject basic to the church function of education.

Criterion—A measure or means for judging or evaluating.

Curriculum—A plan for guiding learning experiences in specific content areas to achieve the church's objectives.

Education—The process by which persons grow in understanding, form new attitudes, and develop actions consistent with the example of Christ.

Educational organization—A structured approach to learning. Such an organization has a philosophy, objectives, programed learning activities, and leaders to conduct these activities. It has a clearly defined constituency and content areas which are properly related to those of other church educational organizations.

Emphasis—An accentuated stress by use of additional resources such as talents, time, or money.

Evaluate—To review what has been accomplished toward reaching desired goals and to judge the value of past action.

Function—A natural characteristic without which the basic nature of an organism would be altered.

Goal—An outcome that may be measured in terms of progress toward an objective through specifically planned action.

Minister—To minister to persons; to make a loving response to the needs of persons in Jesus' name.

Objective—A statement setting forth an ultimate end which a congregation hopes to accomplish.

Organization—The formal arrangement or pattern whereby church members relate themselves to one another for accomplishing specific church tasks.

Plan—The process of determining the future action necessary to accomplish specific goals and objectives. Long-range planning involves determining future action on a five to ten-year basis.

Polity—The principles of government used by a church to organize and operate.

Priority—The order of preference based on the importance in achieving goals and objectives.

Proclaim—To proclaim the gospel; to declare what God has done in and through Jesus Christ for the salvation of men.

Program—Any basic continuing activity which has primary importance in achieving the objectives of the church.

Programing—The process of planning in detail a basic continuing activity.

Program service—A basic continuing activity which enriches or supports the programs of a church.

Project—An activity with a recognizable beginning and ending time. Projects should support programs.

Resources—Those means available to the church for accomplishing its objectives. The Holy Spirit is the chief resource of every church. Other resources are the talents (people), time, money, and facilities.

Scheduling—The arrangement of time for activities on the church calendar in a significant and orderly manner.

Study program—A basic content area which requires continuing study on the part of the congregation in achieving the church's objectives.

Task—A basic responsibility of a church which carries with it the obligation of performance. Tasks may be grouped together to form a program.

Worship—Worship is the experience which is characterized by an awareness of God, a recognition of his holiness and majesty, and a response in loving obedience to his leadership.